The 30 Minute

MEDITERRANEAN

Cookbook

101 HEALTHY, DELICIOUS MEALS FOR
BUSY AND PRODUCTIVE PEOPLE.

MEGAN FLOUR

Disclaimer

This publication is designed to provide competent and reliable information regarding the subject matter covered. However, it is sold with the understanding that the author
is not engaged in rendering professional or nutritional advice. Laws and practices often vary from state and country to country and if medical or other expert assistance is required, the services of a professional should be sought. The author specifically disclaims any liability that is
incurred from use or application of the content of this book.

TABLE OF CONTENTS

MEDITERRANEAN DIET

The Mediterranean diet is inspired by the eating habits of the populations that around the Mediterranean Sea.

The populations of southern Italy and Greece are the main regions that influence this diet. If you decide to follow the Mediterranean diet, the establishment of your diet will be natural products, vegetables, entire grain pieces of bread, pasta, rice, grains, and potatoes, alongside beans, nuts, vegetables, and seeds.

"you are what you eat." If you eat well-balanced, nutritious meals made from natural whole foods then your body will thank you by performing at its best.

The many health benefits tied to this eating lifestyle include reduced risk of:

Alzheimer's disease;

Arthritis;

Asthma;

Cancer;

Cardiovascular disease;

Diabetes;

High cholesterol;

This diet will work well for someone who wants to boost their heart well-being, reduce their cholesterol, lose some weight, and do without feeling insulted as such.

While each of these recipes takes around 30 minutes or less, keep in mind that the prep and cooking times are our best estimates.

In this book, I have included 101 of my favorite 30 MINUTE Mediterranean diet recipes for breakfast, lunch, dinner, snack, dessert and pizza…

Start your day in 30 minute the Mediterranean way with healthy, nutritious meals that will give you a boost of energy for living each day to the fullest!

WRAPPED PLUMS

Total time: 5 minutes

Preparation Time: 5 minutes
Cooking Time: 0 minutes
Servings: 8

Ingredients:
- 2 ounces prosciutto, cut into
- 16 pieces
- 4 plums, quartered
- 1 tablespoon chives, chopped
- A pinch of red pepper flakes, crushed

Directions:
1. Wrap each plum quarter in a prosciutto slice, arrange them all on a platter, sprinkle the chives and pepper flakes all over and serve.

Nutrition:
- Calories 30
- Fat 1g
- Carbohydrates 4g
- Protein 2g

Total time: 5 minutes

Preparation Time: 5 Minutes
Cooking Time: 0 Minutes
Servings: 1

Ingredients:
- 1 cup Dried figs
- 1 cup Kalamata olives
- ½ cup Water
- 1 tbsp Chopped fresh thyme
- 1 tbsp extra virgin olive oil
- ½ tsp Balsamic vinegar

Directions:
1. Prepare figs in a food processor until well chopped, add water, and continue processing to form a paste.
2. Add olives and pulse until well blended.
3. Add thyme, vinegar, and extra virgin olive oil and pulse until very smooth.
4. Best served with crackers of your choice.

Nutrition:
- Calories: 249
- Carbs: 64g
- Fat: 1g
- Protein: 3g

Total time: 5 minutes

Preparation time: 5 minutes
Cooking time: 0 minutes
Servings: 2

Ingredients:
- 2 cucumbers, chopped
- 1 tablespoon olive oil
- Salt and black pepper to the taste
- 1 red chili pepper, dried
- 1 tablespoon lemon juice
- 3 tablespoons walnuts, chopped
- 1 tablespoon balsamic vinegar
- 1 teaspoon chives, chopped

Directions:
1. In a bowl, mix the cucumbers with the oil and the rest of the ingredients, toss and serve as a side dish.

Nutrition:
- calories 121,
- fat 2.3,
- fiber 2.0,
- carbs 6.7,
- protein 2.4

Total Time: 5 minutes

Preparation Time: 5 minutes
Cooking Time: 0 minutes
Servings: 4

Ingredients:
- 2 cups almond milk
- 2 cups quinoa, already cooked
- ½ tsp cinnamon powder
- 1 tbsp. honey
- 1 cup blueberries
- ¼ cup walnuts, chopped

Directions:
1. In a bowl, mix the quinoa with the milk and the rest of the ingredients, toss, divide into smaller bowls.
2. Serve for breakfast.

Nutrition:
- Calories: 284
- Fat: 14.3g
- Carbs: 15.4g
- Protein: 4.4g

ENDIVES, FENNEL AND ORANGE SALAD

Total Time: 5 minutes

Preparation Time: 5 minutes
Cooking Time: 0 minutes
Servings: 4

Ingredients:
- 1 tbsp. balsamic vinegar
- 2 garlic cloves, minced
- 1 tsp. Dijon mustard
- 2 tbsps. olive oil
- 1 tbsp. lemon juice
- Sea salt and black pepper to taste
- ½ cup black olives, pitted and chopped
- 1 tbsp. parsley, chopped
- 7 cups baby spinach
- 2 endives, shredded
- 3 medium navel oranges, peeled and cut into segments
- 2 bulbs fennel, shredded

Directions:
1. In a salad bowl, combine the spinach with the endives, oranges, fennel, and the rest of the ingredients, toss.
2. Serve for breakfast.

Nutrition:
- Calories: 97
- Fat: 9.1g
- Carbs: 3.7g
- Protein: 1.9g

Total time: 5 minutes

Preparation Time: 5 Minutes
Cooking Time: 0 Minutes
Servings: 3

Ingredients:
- 7 pita bread cut into 6 wedges each
- 1 (7 ounces) container plain hummus
- 1 tbsp Greek vinaigrette
- ½ cup Chopped pitted Kalamata olives

Directions:
1. Spread the hummus on a serving plate—
2. Mix vinaigrette and olives in a bowl and spoon over the hummus.
3. Enjoy with wedges of pita bread.

Nutrition:
- Calories: 225
- Carbs: 40g
- Fat: 5g
- Protein: 9g

Total Time: 5 minutes

Preparation time: 5 minutes
Cooking time: 0 minutes
Servings: 1

Ingredients:
- 6 oz. nonfat plain Greek yogurt
- 1/2 cup fresh berries of your choice
- 1 tbsp .25 oz crushed walnuts
- 1 tbsp honey

Directions:
1. In a jar with a lid, add the yogurt.
2. Top with berries and a drizzle of honey.
3. Top with the lid and store in the fridge for 2-3 days.

Nutrition:
- Calories: 250
- Carbs: 35
- Fat: 4g
- Protein: 19g

Total Time: 5 minutes

Preparation Time: 5 minutes
Cooking Time: 0 minutes
Servings: 4

Ingredients:
- 4 cups Greek yogurt, fat-free, plain or vanilla
- ½ cup California walnuts, toasted, chopped
- 3 tbsps. honey or agave nectar
- Fresh fruit, chopped or granola, low-fat (both optional)

Directions:
1. Spoon yogurt into 4 individual cups.
2. Sprinkle 2 tbsps. of walnuts over each and drizzle
3. 2 tsps. of honey over each.
4. Top with fruit or granola, whichever is preferred.

Nutrition:
- Calories: 300
- Fat: 10g
- Carbs: 25g
- Protein: 29g

Total Time: 5 Minutes

Preparation Time: 5 minutes
Cooking Time: 0 minutes
Servings: 2

Ingredients:
- 2 whole-wheat bread slices, toasted
- 1 tsp. water
- 1 tbsp. tahini paste
- 2 tsps. feta cheese, crumbled Juice of ½ lemon
- 2 tsps. pine nuts
- A pinch of black pepper

Directions:
1. In a bowl, mix the tahini with the water and the lemon juice, whisk well, and spread over the toasted bread slices.
2. Top each serving with the remaining ingredients and serve for breakfast.

Nutrition:
- Calories: 142
- Fat: 7.6g
- Carbs: 13.7g
- Protein: 5.8g

MOROCCAN AVOCADO SMOOTHIE

Total Time: 5 minutes

Preparation Time: 5 minutes
Cooking Time: 0 minutes
Servings: 4

Ingredients:
- 1 ripe avocado, peeled and pitted
- 1 overripe banana
- 1 cup almond milk, unsweetened
- 1 cup of ice

Directions:
1. Place the avocado, banana, milk, and ice into your blender.
2. Blend until smooth with no pieces of avocado remaining.

Nutrition:
Calories: 100
Protein: 1 g
Fat: 6 g
Carbohydrates: 11 g

YOGURT DIP

Total time: 10 minutes

Preparation Time: 10 minutes
Cooking Time: 0 minutes
Servings: 6

Ingredients:
- 2 cups Greek yogurt
- 2 tablespoons pistachios, toasted and chopped
- A pinch of salt and white pepper
- 2 tablespoons mint, chopped
- 1 tablespoon kalamata olives, pitted and chopped
- ¼ cup zaatar spice
- ¼ cup pomegranate seeds
- 1/3 cup olive oil

Directions:
1. Mix the yogurt with the pistachios and the rest of the ingredients, whisk well, divide into small cups and serve with pita chips on the side.

Nutrition:
- Calories 294
- Fat 18g
- Carbohydrates 2g
- Protein 10g

LIME CUCUMBER MIX

Total time: 10 minutes

Preparation time: 10 minutes
Cooking time: 0 minutes
Servings: 8

Ingredients:
- 4 cucumbers, chopped
- ½ cup green bell pepper, chopped
- 1 yellow onion, chopped
- 1 chili pepper, chopped
- 1 garlic clove, minced
- 1 teaspoon parsley, chopped
- 2 tablespoons lime juice
- 1 tablespoon dill, chopped
- Salt and black pepper to the taste
- 1 tablespoon olive oil

Directions:
1. In a large bowl, mix the cucumber with the bell peppers and the rest of the ingredients, toss and serve as a side dish.

Nutrition:
- calories 123,
- fat 4.3,
- fiber 2.3,
- carbs 5.6,
- protein 2

HONEY ALMOND RICOTTA SPREAD WITH PEACHES

Total Time: 13 minutes

Preparation Time: 5 minutes
Cooking Time: 8 minutes
Servings: 4

Ingredients:
- 1/2 cup Fisher Sliced Almonds
- 1 cup whole milk ricotta 1
- /4 teaspoon almond extract zest from an orange, optional
- 1 teaspoon honey hearty whole-grain toast
- English muffin or bagel extra
- Fisher sliced almonds sliced peaches extra honey for drizzling

Directions:
1. Cut peaches into a proper shape and then brush them with olive oil.
2. After that, set it aside. Take a bowl; combine the ingredients for the filling. Set aside.
3. Then just pre-heat grill to medium.
4. Place peaches cut side down onto the greased grill.
5. Close lid cover and then just grill until the peaches have softened, approximately 6-10 minutes, depending on the size of the peaches.
6. Then you will have to place peach halves onto a serving plate.
7. Put a spoon of about 1 tablespoon of ricotta mixture into the cavity (you are also allowed to use a small scooper).
8. Sprinkle it with slivered almonds, crushed amaretti cookies, and honey.
9. Decorate with the mint leaves.

Nutrition:
- Calories: 187
- Protein: 7 g
- Fat: 9 g
- Carbs: 18 g

SMOKED SALMON AND POACHED EGGS ON TOAST

Total Time: 14 minutes

Preparation Time: 10 minutes
Cooking Time: 4 minutes
Servings: 4

Ingredients:
- 2 oz avocado smashed
- 2 slices of bread toasted
- Pinch of kosher salt and cracked black pepper
- 1/4 tsp freshly squeezed lemon juice
- 2 eggs see notes, poached
- 3.5 oz smoked salmon
- 1 tbsp. thinly sliced scallions
- Splash of Kikkoman soy sauce optional
- Microgreens are optional

Directions:
1. Take a small bowl and then smash the avocado into it.
2. Then, add the lemon juice and also a pinch of salt into the mixture. Then, mix it well and set aside.
3. After that, poach the eggs and toast the bread for some time.
4. Once the bread is toasted, you will have to spread the avocado on both slices and after that, add the smoked salmon to each slice.
5. Thereafter, carefully transfer the poached eggs to the respective toasts.
6. Add a splash of Kikkoman soy sauce and some cracked pepper; then, just garnish with scallions and microgreens.

Nutrition:
- Calories: 459
- Protein: 31 g
- Fat: 22 g
- Carbs: 33 g

BLUEBERRY, HAZELNUT, AND LEMON BREAKFAST GRAIN SALAD

Total Time: 15 minutes

Preparation Time: 5 minutes
Cooking Time: 10 minutes
Servings: 8

Ingredients:
- 1 cup steel-cut oats
- 1 cup dry golden quinoa
- ½ cup dry millet
- 3 tbsps. olive oil, divided
- ¾ tsp salt 1 x 1" piece fresh ginger, peeled and cut into coins
- 2 large lemons, zest and juice
- ½ cup maple syrup
- 1 cup Greek yogurt
- ¼ tsp nutmeg
- 2 cups hazelnuts, roughly chopped and toasted
- 2 cups blueberries or mixed berries 4
- ½ cups water

Directions:
1. Grab a mesh strainer and add the oats, quinoa, and millet.
2. Wash well then pop to one side.
3. Find a 3-quart saucepan, add a tbsp of the oil, and pop over medium heat.
4. Add the grains and cook for 2-3 minutes to toast.
5. Pour in the water, salt, ginger coins, and lemon zest.
6. Bring to the boil then cover and turn down the heat.
7. Leave to simmer for 20 minutes.
8. Turn off the heat and leave to sit for five minutes.
9. Fluff with a fork, remove the ginger then leave to cool for at least an hour.
10. Grab a large bowl and add the grains.
11. Take a medium bowl and add the remaining olive oil, lemon juice, maple syrup, yogurt, and nutmeg.
12. Whisk well to combine.
13. Pour this over the grains and stir well.

14. Add the hazelnuts and blueberries, stir again then pop into the fridge overnight.
15. Serve and enjoy.

Nutrition:
- Calories: 363
- Fat: 11g
- Carbs: 60g
- Protein: 7g

Total Time: 15 minutes

Preparation Time: 10 minutes
Cooking Time: 5 minutes
Servings: 2

Ingredients:
- 2 (6- to 7-inch) whole-wheat submarine or hoagie rolls, sliced open horizontally
- 1 tablespoon extra-virgin olive oil
- 1 garlic clove, halved
- 1 large ripe tomato, cut into
- 8 slices
- ¼ teaspoon dried oregano
- 1 cup fresh mozzarella (about 4 ounces), patted dry and sliced
- ¼ cup lightly packed fresh basil leaves, torn into small pieces
- ¼ teaspoon freshly ground black pepper

Directions:
1. Preheat the broiler to high with the rack 4 inches under the heating element.
2. Place the sliced bread on a large, rimmed baking sheet.
3. Place under the broiler for 1 minute, until the bread is just lightly toasted.
4. Remove from the oven.
5. Brush each piece of the toasted bread with the oil, and rub a garlic half over each piece.
6. Place the toasted bread back on the baking sheet.
7. Evenly distribute the tomato slices on each piece, sprinkle with the oregano, and layer the cheese on top.
8. Place the baking sheet under the broiler.
9. Set the timer for 1½ minutes but check after 1 minute.
10. When the cheese is melted and the edges are just starting to get dark brown, remove the sandwiches from the oven (this can take anywhere from 1½ to 2 minutes).
11. Top each sandwich with the fresh basil and pepper.

Nutrition:
- Calories 297;
- Total Fat: 11g;

- Saturated Fat: 5g;
- Cholesterol: 22mg;
- Sodium: 450mg;
- Total Carbohydrates: 38g;
- Fiber: 4g;
- Protein: 12g

Total time: 15 minutes

Preparation Time: 15 Minutes
Cooking Time: 0 Minutes
Servings: 4

Ingredients:
- 1 large Sweet potato
- 1 tbsp Extra virgin olive oil
- Salt

Directions:
1. 300°F preheated oven.
2. Slice your potato into nice, thin slices that resemble fries.
3. Toss the potato slices with salt and extra virgin olive oil in a bowl.
4. Bake for about one hour, flipping every 15 minutes until crispy and browned.

Nutrition:
- Calories: 150
- Carbs: 16g
- Fat: 9g
- Protein: 1g

Total time: 15 minutes

Preparation Time: 10 minutes
Cooking Time: 5 minutes
Servings: 4

Ingredients:
- ¼ cup dried cranberries
- ¼ cup extra virgin olive oil
- ¼ cup olive oil
- ¼ cup sliced almonds
- ½ lemon, juiced
- ¾ cup blueberries
- 1 ½ lb. calamari tube, cleaned
- 1 granny smith apple, sliced thinly
- 1 tbsp. fresh lemon juice
- 2 tbsp. apple cider vinegar
- 6 cups fresh spinach Freshly grated pepper to taste
- Sea salt to taste

Directions:
1. In a small bowl, make the vinaigrette by mixing well the tbsp. of lemon juice, apple cider vinegar, and extra virgin olive oil.
2. Season with pepper and salt to taste.
3. Set aside.
4. Turn on the grill to medium fire and let the grates heat up for a minute or two.
5. In a large bowl, add olive oil and the calamari tube.
6. Season calamari generously with pepper and salt.
7. Place seasoned and oiled calamari onto heated grate and grill until cooked or opaque.
8. This is around two minutes per side.
9. As you wait for the calamari to cook, you can combine almonds, cranberries, blueberries, spinach, and the thinly sliced apple in a large salad bowl.
10. Toss to mix.
11. Remove cooked calamari from grill and transfer on a chopping board.
12. Cut into ¼-inch thick rings and throw into the salad bowl.

13. Drizzle with vinaigrette and toss well to coat salad.
14. Serve and enjoy!

Nutrition:
- Calories: 567;
- Fat: 24.5g;
- Protein: 54.8g;   Carbs: 30.6g

BAKED COD CRUSTED WITH HERBS

Total time: 15 minutes

Preparation Time: 5 minutes
Cooking Time: 10 minutes
Servings: 4

Ingredients:
- ¼ cup honey
- ¼ tsp.
- salt
- ½ cup panko
- ½ tsp. pepper
- 1 tbsp. extra virgin olive oil
- 1 tbsp. lemon juice
- 1 tsp. dried basil
- 1 tsp. dried parsley
- 1 tsp. rosemary
- 4 pieces of 4-oz cod fillets

Directions:
1. With olive oil, grease a 9 x 13-inch baking pan and preheat oven to 375oF.
2. In a zip top bag mix panko, rosemary, salt, pepper, parsley and basil.
3. Evenly spread cod fillets in prepped dish and drizzle with lemon juice.
4. Then brush the fillets with honey on all sides.
5. Discard remaining honey if any.
6. Then evenly divide the panko mixture on top of cod fillets.
7. Pop in the oven and bake for ten minutes or until fish is cooked.
8. Serve and enjoy.

Nutrition:
- Calories: 137;
- Protein: 5g;
- Fat: 2g;
- Carbs: 21g

GREEK YOGURT PANCAKES

Total Time: 15 minutes

Preparation Time: 10 minutes
Cooking Time: 5 minutes
Servings: 2

Ingredients:
- 1 cup all-purpose flour
- 1 cup whole-wheat flour
- 1/4 teaspoon salt
- 4 teaspoons baking powder
- 1 tablespoon sugar
- 1 ½ cups unsweetened almond milk
- 2 teaspoons vanilla extract
- 2 large eggs
- 1/2 cup plain
- 2% Greek yogurt
- Fruit, for serving
- Maple syrup, for serving

Directions:
1. First, you will have to pour the curds into the bowl and mix them well until creamy.
2. After that, you will have to add egg whites and mix them well until combined.
3. Then take a separate bowl, pour the wet mixture into the dry mixture.
4. Stir to combine. The batter will be extremely thick.
5. Then, simply spoon the batter onto the sprayed pan heated too medium-high.
6. The batter must make 4 large pancakes.
7. Then, you will have to flip the pancakes once when they start to bubble a bit on the surface. Cook until golden brown on both sides.

Nutrition:
- Calories: 166
- Protein: 14 g
- Fat: 5 g
- Carbs: 52g

Total time: 15 minutes

Preparation Time: 5 Minutes
Cooking Time: 10 Minutes
Servings: 2

Ingredients:
- 1 Butternut squash
- 1 tbsp Extra virgin olive oil
- ½ tbsp Grapeseed oil
- 1/8 tsp Sea
- salt

Directions:
1. Remove seeds from the squash and cut into thin slices.
2. Coat with extra virgin olive oil and grapeseed oil.
3. Add a sprinkle of salt and toss to coat well.
4. Arrange the squash slices onto three baking sheets and bake for 10 minutes until crispy.

Nutrition:
- Calories: 40
- Carbs: 10g
- Fat: 0g
- Protein: 1g

COCONUT SALSA ON CHIPOTLE FISH TACOS

Total time: 20 minutes

Preparation Time: 10 minutes
Cooking Time: 10 minutes
Servings: 4

Ingredients:
- ¼ cup chopped fresh cilantro
- ½ cup seeded and finely chopped plum tomato
- 1 cup peeled and finely chopped mango
- 1 lime cut into wedges
- 1 tbsp. chipotle Chile powder
- 1 tbsp. safflower oil
- 1/3 cup finely chopped red onion
- 10 tbsp. fresh lime juice, divided
- 4 6-oz boneless, skinless cod fillets
- 5 tbsp. dried unsweetened shredded coconut
- 8 pcs of 6-inch tortillas, heated

Directions:
1. Whisk well Chile powder, oil, and
2. 4 tbsp. lime juice in a glass baking dish.
3. Add cod and marinate for 12 – 15 minutes.
4. Turning once halfway through the marinating time.
5. Make the salsa by mixing coconut, 6 tbsp. lime juice, cilantro, onions, tomatoes and mangoes in a medium bowl. Set aside.
6. On high, heat a grill pan.
7. Place cod and grill for four minutes per side turning only once.
8. Once cooked, slice cod into large flakes and evenly divide onto tortilla.
9. Evenly divide salsa on top of cod and serve with a side of lime wedges.

Nutrition:
- Calories: 477;
- Protein: 35.0g;
- Fat: 12.4g;
- Carbs: 57.4g

OVERNIGHT BERRY CHIA OATS

Total Time: 20 minutes

Preparation time: 15 minutes
Cooking time: 5 minutes
Servings: 1

Ingredients:
- 1/2 cup Quaker Oats rolled oats
- 1/4 cup chia seeds
- 1 cup milk or water pinch of salt and cinnamon maple syrup, or a different sweetener, to taste
- 1 cup frozen berries of choice or smoothie leftovers

Toppings:
- Yogurt Berries

Directions:
1. In a jar with a lid, add the oats, seeds, milk, salt, and cinnamon, refrigerate overnight.
2. On serving day, puree the berries in a blender.
3. Stir the oats, add in the berry puree and top with yogurt and more berries, nuts, honey, or garnish of your choice.
4. Enjoy!

Nutrition:
- Calories: 405
- Carbs: 65g
- Fat: 11g
- Protein: 17g

Total time: 25 minutes

Preparation Time: 10 minutes
Cooking Time: 15 minutes
Servings: 2

Ingredients:
- 1 (15-ounce) can chickpeas, drained and rinsed
- ½ cup Lemony Garlic Hummus or ½ cup prepared hummus
- ½ cup whole-wheat panko bread crumbs
- 1 large egg
- 2 teaspoons dried oregano
- ¼ teaspoon freshly ground black pepper
- 1 tablespoon extra-virgin olive oil
- 1 cucumber, unpeeled (or peeled if desired), cut in half lengthwise
- 1 (6-ounce) container
- 2% plain Greek yogurt
- 1 garlic clove, minced (about ½ teaspoon)
- 2 whole-wheat pita breads, cut in half
- 1 medium tomato, cut into 4 thick slices

Directions:
1. In a large bowl, mash the chickpeas with a potato masher or fork until coarsely smashed (they should still be somewhat chunky).
2. Add the hummus, bread crumbs, egg, oregano, and pepper.
3. Stir well to combine.
4. With your hands, form the mixture into 4 (½-cup-size) patties.
5. Press each patty flat to about ¾ inch thick and put on a plate.
6. In a large skillet over medium-high heat, heat the oil until very hot, about 3 minutes.
7. Cook the patties for 5 minutes, then flip with a spatula.
8. Cook for an additional 5 minutes.
9. While the patties are cooking, shred half of the cucumber with a box grater or finely chop with a knife.
10. In a small bowl, stir together the shredded cucumber, yogurt, and garlic to make the tzatziki sauce.
11. Slice the remaining half of the cucumber into ¼-inch-thick slices and set aside.

12. Toast the pita breads.
13. To assemble the sandwiches, lay the pita halves on a work surface.
14. Into each pita, place a few slices of cucumber, a chickpea patty, and a tomato slice, then drizzle the sandwich with the tzatziki sauce and serve.

Nutrition:
- Calories: 375;
- Total Fat: 12g;
- Saturated Fat: 2g;
- Cholesterol: 49mg;
- Sodium: 632mg;
- Total Carbohydrates: 53g;
- Fiber: 10g;
- Protein: 17g

DATE AND WALNUT OVERNIGHT OATS

Total Time: 25 minutes

Preparation Time: 5 minutes
Cooking Time: 20 minutes
Servings: 2

Ingredients:
- ¼ Cup Greek Yogurt, Plain
- 1/3 cup of yogurt
- 2/3 cup of oats
- 1 cup of milk
- 2 tsp date syrup or you can also use maple syrup or honey
- 1 mashed banana
- ¼ tsp cinnamon
- ¼ cup walnuts
- Pinch of salt (approx.1/8 tsp)

Directions:
1. Get a mason jar or a small bowl and add all the ingredients.
2. After that stir and mix all the ingredients well.
3. Cover it securely, and cool it in a refrigerator overnight.
4. Take it out the next morning, add more liquid or cinnamon if required.
5. Serve cold.

Nutrition:
- Calories: 350
- Protein: 14 g
- Fat: 12 g
- Carbs: 49 g

MEDITERRANEAN EGGS WHITE BREAKFAST SANDWICH WITH ROASTED TOMATOES

Total Time: 25 minutes

Preparation Time: 15 minutes
Cooking Time: 10 minutes
Servings: 2

Ingredients:
- Salt and pepper to taste
- ¼ cup egg whites
- 1 teaspoon chopped fresh herbs like rosemary, basil, parsley,
- 1 whole-grain seeded ciabatta roll
- 1 teaspoon butter
- 1-2 slices Muenster cheese
- 1 tablespoon pesto
- About ½ cup roasted tomatoes
- 10 ounces grape tomatoes
- 1 tablespoon extra-virgin olive oil
- Black pepper and salt to taste

Directions:
1. First, you will have to melt the butter over medium heat in the small nonstick skillet.
2. Then, mix the egg whites with pepper and salt.
3. Then, sprinkle it with the fresh herbs. After that cook it for almost 3-4 minutes or until the eggs are done, then flip it carefully.
4. Meanwhile, toast ciabatta bread in the toaster.
5. Place the egg on the bottom half of the sandwich rolls, then top with cheese
6. Add roasted tomatoes and the top half of roll.
7. To make a roasted tomato, preheat the oven to 400 degrees.
8. Then, slice the tomatoes in half lengthwise.
9. Place on the baking sheet and drizzle with olive oil.
10. Season it with pepper and salt and then roast in the oven for about 20 minutes.
11. Skins will appear wrinkled when done.

Nutrition:

- Calories: 458
- Protein: 21 g
- Fat: 24 g
- Carbs: 51 g

FETA - AVOCADO & MASHED CHICKPEA TOAST

Total Time: 25 minutes

Preparation Time: 10 minutes
Cooking Time: 15 minutes
Servings: 4

Ingredients:
- 15 oz. can
- Chickpeas 2 oz.
- ½ cup Diced feta cheese
- 1 Pitted avocado
Fresh juice:
- 2 tsp. Lemon (or 1 tbsp. orange)
- ½ tsp. Black pepper
- 2 tsp. Honey 4 slices
- Multigrain toast

Directions:
- Toast the bread.
- Drain the chickpeas in a colander.
- Scoop the avocado flesh into the bowl. Use a large fork/potato masher to mash them until the mix is spreadable.
- Pour in the lemon juice, pepper, and feta.
- Combine and divide onto the four slices of toast.
- Drizzle using the honey and serve.

Nutrition:
- Calories: 337
- Carbs: 43g
- Fat: 13g
- Protein: 13g

LOW-CARB BAKED EGGS WITH AVOCADO AND FETA

Total Time: 25 minutes

Preparation Time: 10 minutes
Cooking Time: 15 minutes
Servings: 2

Ingredients:
- 1 avocado
- 4 eggs
- 2-3 tbsp. crumbled feta cheese
- Nonstick cooking spray
- Pepper and salt to taste

Directions:
1. First, you will have to preheat the oven to 400 degrees f.
2. After that, when the oven is on the proper temperature, you will have to put the gratin dishes right on the baking sheet.
3. Then, leave the dishes to heat in the oven for almost 10 minutes
4. After that process, you need to break the eggs into individual ramekins.
5. Then, let the avocado and eggs come to room temperature for at least 10 minutes.
6. Then, peel the avocado properly and cut it each half into 6-8 slices.
7. You will have to remove the dishes from the oven and spray them with the non-stick spray.
8. Then, you will have to arrange all the sliced avocados in the dishes and tip two eggs into each dish.
9. Sprinkle with feta, add pepper and salt to taste
10. Serve.

Nutrition:
- Calories: 280
- Protein: 11 g
- Fat: 23 g
- Carbs: 10 g

Total Time: 30 minutes

Preparation time: 15 minutes
Cooking time: 15 minutes
Servings: 6

Ingredients:

- 9 Slices of thin cut deli ham
- 1/2 cup canned roasted red pepper, sliced + additional for garnish
- 1/3 cup fresh spinach, minced
- 1/4 cup feta cheese, crumbled
- 5 large eggs
- Pinch of salt
- Pinch of pepper
- 1 1/2 tbsp Pesto sauce Fresh basil for garnish

Directions:

1. Preheat oven to 400 degrees F.
2. Spray a muffin tin with cooking spray, generously.
3. Line each of the muffin tin with 1 ½ pieces of ham - making sure there aren't any holes for the egg mixture come out.
4. Place some of the roasted red pepper in the bottom of each muffin tin.
5. Place 1 tbsp of minced spinach on top of each red pepper.
6. Top the pepper and spinach off with a large 1/2 tbsp of crumbled feta cheese.
7. In a medium bowl, whisk together the eggs salt and pepper, divide the egg mixture evenly among the 6 muffin tins.
8. Bake for 15 to 17 minutes until the eggs are puffy and set.
9. Remove each cup from the muffin tin. Allow to cool completely Distribute the muffins among the containers, store in the fridge for 2 - 3days or in the freezer for 3 months.

Nutrition:

- Calories: 109
- Carbs: 2g
- Fat: 6g

- Protein: 9g

MEDITERRANEAN EGGS CUPS

Total Time: 30 minutes

Preparation Time: 10 minutes
Cooking Time: 20 minutes
Servings: 8

Ingredients:
- 1 cup spinach, finely diced
- 1/2 yellow onion, finely diced
- 1/2 cup sliced sun-dried tomatoes
- 4 large basil leaves, finely diced
- Pepper and salt to taste
- 1/3 cup feta cheese crumbles
- 8 large eggs
- 1/4 cup milk (any kind)

Directions:
1. Warm the oven to 375°F.
2. Then, roll the dough sheet into a 12x8-inch rectangle.
3. Then, cut in half lengthwise.
4. After that, you will have to cut each half crosswise into 4 pieces, forming 8 (4x3-inch) pieces dough.
5. Then, press each into the bottom and up sides of the ungreased muffin cup.
6. Trim dough to keep the dough from touching, if essential. Set aside.
7. Then, you will have to combine the eggs, salt, pepper in the bowl and beat it with a whisk until well mixed. Set aside.
8. Melt the butter in 12-inch skillet over medium heat until sizzling; add bell peppers.
9. You will have to cook it, stirring occasionally, 2-3 minutes or until crisply tender.
10. After that, add spinach leaves; continue cooking until spinach is wilted. Then just add egg mixture and prosciutto.
11. Divide the mixture evenly among prepared muffin cups.
12. Bake it for 14-17 minutes or until the crust is golden brown.

Nutrition:
- Calories: 240
- Protein: 9 g

- Fat: 16 g
- Carbs: 13 g

TUNA AND COUSCOUS

Total Time: 10 minutes

Preparation time: 10 minutes
Cooking time: 0 minutes
Servings: 4

Ingredients:
- 1 cup chicken stock
- 1 and ¼ cups couscous
- A pinch of salt and black pepper
- 10 ounces canned tuna, drained and flaked
- 1-pint cherry tomatoes, halved
- ½ cup pepperoncini, sliced
- 1/3 cup parsley, chopped
- 1 tablespoon olive oil
- ¼ cup capers, drained Juice of ½ lemon

Directions:
1. Put the stock in a pan, bring to a boil over medium-high heat, add the couscous, stir, take off the heat, cover, leave aside for 10 minutes, fluff with a fork and transfer to a bowl.
2. Add the tuna and the rest of the ingredients, toss and serve for lunch right away.

Nutrition:
- Calories: 253
- Fat: 11.5,
- Fiber: 3.4,
- Carbs: 16.5
- Protein: 23.2

CHICKEN STUFFED PEPPERS

Total Time: 10 minutes

Preparation time: 10 minutes
Cooking time: 0 minutes
Servings: 6

Ingredients:
- 1 cup Greek yogurt
- 2 tablespoons mustard
- Salt and black pepper to the taste
- 1-pound rotisserie chicken meat, cubed
- 4 celery stalks, chopped
- 2 tablespoons balsamic vinegar
- 1 bunch scallions, sliced
- ¼ cup parsley, chopped
- 1 cucumber, sliced
- 3 red bell peppers, halved and deseeded
- 1-pint cherry tomatoes, quartered

Directions:
1. In a bowl, mix the chicken with the celery and the rest of the ingredients except the bell peppers and toss well.
2. Stuff the peppers halves with the chicken mix and serve for lunch.

Nutrition:
- calories 266,
- fat 12.2,
- fiber 4.5,
- carbs 15.7,
- protein 3.7

EGG WHITE SCRAMBLE WITH CHERRY TOMATOES & SPINACH

Total Time: 13-15 minutes

Preparation Time: 5 minutes
Cooking Time: 8-10 minutes
Servings: 4

Ingredients:
- 1 tbsp. Olive oil
- 1 whole Egg
- 10 Egg whites
- ¼ tsp.
- Black pepper
- ½ tsp.
- Salt
- 1 garlic clove, minced
- 2 cups cherry tomatoes, halved
- 2 cups packed fresh baby spinach
- ½ cup Light cream or Half & Half
- ¼ cup finely grated parmesan cheese

Directions:
1. Whisk the eggs, pepper, salt, and milk.
2. Prepare a skillet using the med-high temperature setting.
3. Toss in the garlic when the pan is hot to sauté for approximately 30 seconds.
4. Pour in the tomatoes and spinach and continue to sauté it for one additional minute.
5. The tomatoes should be softened, and the spinach wilted.
6. Add the egg mixture into the pan using the medium heat setting.
7. Fold the egg gently as it cooks for about two to three minutes.
8. Remove from the burner, and sprinkle with a sprinkle of cheese.

Nutrition:
- Calories 142
- Protein: 15g
- Fat: 2g
- Carbs 4g

BROCCOLI AND CARROT PASTA SALAD

Total time: 15 minutes

Preparation time: 5 minutes
Cooking time: 10 minutes
Servings: 4

Ingredients:
- 8 ounces (227 g) whole-wheat pasta
- 2 cups broccoli florets
- 1 cup peeled and shredded carrots
- ¼ cup plain Greek yogurt
- Juice of 1 lemon
- 1 teaspoon red pepper flakes
- Sea salt and freshly ground pepper, to taste

Directions:
1. Bring a large pot of lightly salted water to a boil.
2. Add the pasta to the boiling water and cook until al dente, about 8 to 10 minutes.
3. Drain the pasta and let rest for a few minutes.
4. When cooled, combine the pasta with the veggies, yogurt, lemon juice, and red pepper flakes in a large bowl, and stir thoroughly to combine.
5. Taste and season to taste with salt and pepper.
6. Serve immediately.

Nutrition:
- Calories: 428
- Fat: 2.9g
- Protein: 15.9g
- Carbs: 84.6g

Total time: 17 minutes

Preparation Time: 10 minutes
Cooking Time: 7 minutes
Servings: 2

Ingredients:
- ¼ cup raw pine nuts
- 4 cups leftover vegetables
- 2 garlic cloves, minced
- 1 tbsp. extra virgin olive oil
- 4 medium zucchinis, cut into long strips resembling noodles

Directions:
1. Heat oil in a large skillet over medium heat and sauté the garlic for 2 minutes.
2. Add the leftover vegetables and place the zucchini noodles on top.
3. Let it cook for five minutes.
4. Garnish with pine nuts.

Nutrition:
- Calories: 288;
- Carbs: 23.6g;
- Protein: 8.2g;
- Fat: 19.2g

Total time: 20 minutes

Preparation Time: 10 minutes
Cooking Time: 10 minutes
Servings: 2

Ingredients:
- 2 medium-sized zucchinis, cut into thin strips or spaghetti noodles
- Salt and pepper to taste
- 1 lemon, zested and juiced
- 2 garlic cloves, minced
- 2 tbsp. ghee, melted
- 2 tbsp. olive oil
- 8 oz. shrimps, cleaned and deveined

Directions:
1. Preheat the oven to 400°F.
2. In a mixing bowl, mix all ingredients except the zucchini noodles.
3. Toss to coat the shrimp.
4. Bake for 10 minutes until the shrimps turn pink.
5. Add the zucchini pasta then toss.

Nutrition:
- Calories: 299;
- Fat: 23.2g;
- Protein: 14.3g;
- Carbs: 10.9g

Total time: 20 minutes

Preparation time: 10 minutes
Cooking time: 10 minutes
Servings: 4

Ingredients:
- 10 ounces couscous
- 1 and ½ cup hot water
- 2 garlic cloves, minced
- 2 tablespoons olive oil
- ½ cup raisins
- 2 bunches Swiss chard, chopped
- Salt and black pepper to the taste

Directions:
1. Put couscous in a bowl, add the water, stir, cover, leave aside for 10 minutes and fluff with a fork.
2. Heat up a pan with the oil over medium heat, add the garlic, and sauté for 1 minute.
3. Add the couscous and the rest of the ingredients, toss, divide between plates and serve.

Nutrition:
- calories 300,
- fat 6.9,
- fiber 11.4,
- carbs 17.4,
- protein 6

Total time: 20 minutes

Preparation Time: 11 minutes
Cooking Time: 9 minutes
Servings: 4

Ingredients

- 16-ounce package of Penne Pasta
- 1-pound Chicken Breast Halves
- 1/2 cup of Chopped Red Onion
- 1 1/2 tablespoons of Butter
- 2 cloves of Minced Garlic
- 14-ounce can of Artichoke Hearts
- 1 Chopped Tomato
- 3 tablespoons of Chopped Fresh Parsley
- 1/2 cup of Crumbled Feta Cheese
- 2 tablespoons of Lemon Juice
- 1 teaspoon of Dried Oregano Ground
- Black Pepper
- Salt

Directions:

1. In a large sized skillet over a medium-high heat, melt your butter.
2. Add your garlic and onion.
3. Cook approximately 2 minutes.
4. Add your chopped chicken and continue to cook until golden brown.
5. Should take approximately 5 to 6 minutes.
6. Stir occasionally.
7. Reduce your heat to a medium-low.
8. Drain and chop your artichoke hearts.
9. Add them to your skillet along with your chopped tomato, fresh parsley, feta cheese, dried oregano, lemon juice, and drained pasta.
10. Cook for 2 to 3. Season.
11. Serve!

Nutrition:

- 411 calories
- 20g fats
- 8g protein

Total Time: 20 minutes

Preparation time: 5 minutes
Cooking time: 15 minutes
Servings: 4

Ingredients:
- 2 tablespoons of olive oil
- 1 medium-sized onion chopped up
- 3 minced cloves of garlic
- 1 medium-sized red pepper completely deseeded and finely chopped
- 1 cup of tomato puree
- 2 tablespoons of tomato paste
- 1 pound of gnocchi
- 1 cup of coarsely chopped turkey ham
- ½ cup of sliced pitted olives
- 1 teaspoon of Italian seasoning
- Salt as needed
- Freshly ground black pepper
- Bunch of fresh basil leaves

Directions:
1. Take a medium-sized sauce pan and place over medium-high heat.
2. Pour some olive oil and heat it up.
3. Toss in the bell pepper, onion and garlic and sauté for 2 minutes.
4. Pour in the tomato puree, gnocchi, tomato paste and add the turkey ham, Italian seasoning and olives.
5. Simmer the whole mix for 15 minutes, making sure to stir from time to time. Season the mix with some pepper and salt.
6. Once done, transfer the mix to a dish and garnish with some basil leaves.
7. Serve hot.

Nutrition:
- Calories: 335
- Fat: 12g

- Carbohydrates: 45g
- Protein: 15g

CREAMY GARLIC PARMESAN CHICKEN PASTA

Total time: 20 minutes

Preparation time: 5 minutes
Cooking time: 15 minutes
Servings: 4

Ingredients:
- 3 tablespoons extra-virgin olive oil
- 2 boneless, skinless chicken breasts, cut into thin strips
- 1 large onion, thinly sliced
- 3 tablespoons garlic, minced
- 1½ teaspoons salt
- 1 pound (454 g) fettuccine pasta
- 1 cup heavy whipping cream
- ¾ cup freshly grated Parmesan cheese, divided
- ½ teaspoon freshly ground black pepper

Directions:
1. In a large skillet over medium heat, heat the olive oil.
2. Add the chicken and cook for 3 minutes.
3. Add the onion, garlic and salt to the skillet.
4. Cook for 7 minutes, stirring occasionally.
5. Meanwhile, bring a large pot of salted water to a boil and add the pasta, then cook for 7 minutes.
6. While the pasta is cooking, add the heavy cream, ½ cup of the Parmesan cheese and black pepper to the chicken.
7. Simmer for 3 minutes.
8. Reserve ½ cup of the pasta water.
9. Drain the pasta and add it to the chicken cream sauce.
10. Add the reserved pasta water to the pasta and toss together.
11. Simmer for 2 minutes.
12. Top with the remaining ¼ cup of the Parmesan cheese and serve warm.

Nutrition:
- Calories: 879
- Fat: 42.0g

- Protein: 35.0g
- Carbs: 90.0g

Total Time: 20 minutes

Preparation time: 15 minutes
Cooking time: 15 minutes
Servings: 4

Ingredients:
- 2 (15 oz) cans chickpeas, divided
- 2 1/2 tbsp olive oil, divided, plus more for frying 1 cup onion, chopped, about
- 1/2 a small onion 2 tbsp garlic, minced
- 2 cups cauliflower, cut into small pieces, about 1/2 a large head
- 1/2 tsp salt black pepper

Topping:
- Hummus, of choice Green onion, diced

Directions:
1. Preheat oven to 400°F.
2. Rinse and drain 1 can of the chickpeas, place them on a paper towel to dry off well.
3. Then place the chickpeas into a large bowl, removing the loose skins that come off, and toss with 1 tbsp of olive oil, spread the chickpeas onto a large pan and sprinkle with salt and pepper.
4. Bake for 20 minutes, then stir, and then bake an additional 5-10 minutes until very crispy.
5. Once the chickpeas are roasted, transfer them to a large food processor and process until broken down and crumble
6. Don't over process them and turn it into flour, as you need to have some texture.
7. Place the mixture into a small bowl, set aside.
8. In a large pan over medium-high heat, add the remaining 1 1/2 tbsp of olive oil.
9. Once heated, add in the onion and garlic, cook until lightly golden brown, about 2 minutes.
10. Then add in the chopped cauliflower, cook for an additional 2 minutes, until the cauliflower is golden.
11. Turn the heat down to low and cover the pan, cook until the cauliflower is fork tender and the onions are golden brown and caramelized, stirring often, about 3-5 minutes.

12. Transfer the cauliflower mixture to the food processor, drain and rinse the remaining can of chickpeas and add them into the food processor, along with the salt and a pinch of pepper.
13. Blend until smooth, and the mixture starts to ball, stop to scrape down the sides as needed
14. Transfer the cauliflower mixture into a large bowl and add in 1/2 cup of the roasted chickpea crumbs, stir until well combined.
15. In a large bowl over medium heat, add in enough oil to lightly cover the bottom of a large pan.
16. Working in batches, cook the patties until golden brown, about 2-3 minutes, flip and cook again.
17. Serve.

Nutrition:
- Calories: 333
- Carbohydrates: 45g
- Fat: 13g
- Protein: 14g

Total Time: 20 minutes

Preparation time: 15 minutes
Cooking time: 5 minutes
Servings: 4

Ingredients:
- 1 eggplant, cut into 1-inch pieces
- ½ cup of water
- ¼ cup Can tomato, crushed
- ½ teaspoon Italian seasoning
- 1 teaspoon paprika
- ½ teaspoon chili powder
- 1 teaspoon garlic powder
- 2 tablespoons olive oil
- Salt

Directions:
1. Add water and eggplant into the instant pot.
2. Seal pot with lid and cook on high for 5 minutes.
3. Once done, release pressure using quick release.
4. Remove lid.
5. Drain eggplant well and clean the instant pot.
6. Add oil into the inner pot of the instant pot and set the pot on sauté mode.
7. Add eggplant along with remaining ingredients and stir well and cook for 5 minutes.
8. Serve.

Nutrition:
- Calories: 97
- Fat: 7.5 g
- Carbs: 8.2 g
- Protein: 1.5 g

TOMATO PORK PASTE

Total time: 20-23 minutes

Preparation Time: 5-8 minutes
Cooking Time: 15 minutes
Servings: 4

Ingredients:
- 2 cups tomato puree
- 1 tablespoon red wine
- 1-pound lean ground pork
- 8-10-ounce pack paste of your choice, uncooked
- Salt and black pepper to taste
- 1 tablespoon vegetable oil

Directions:
1. Season the pork with black pepper and salt.
2. Place your instant pot over a dry kitchen platform.
3. Open the top lid and plug it on.
4. Press "SAUTE" Cooking function; add the oil and heat it.
5. In the pot, add the ground meat; stir-cook using wooden spatula until turns evenly brown for 8-10 minutes.
6. Add the wine. Cook for 1-2 minutes.
7. Add the ingredients; gently stir to mix well.
8. Properly close the top lid; make sure that the safety valve is properly locked.
9. Press "MEAT/STEW" Cooking function; set pressure level to "HIGH" and set the Cooking time to 6 minutes.
10. Allow the pressure to build to cook the ingredients.
11. After Cooking time is over press "CANCEL" setting. Find and press "NPR" Cooking function.
12. This setting is for the natural release of inside pressure, and it takes around 10 minutes to slowly release pressure.
13. Slowly open the lid, take out the cooked recipe in serving containers.
14. Serve warm.

Nutrition:
- Calories: 423

- Protein: 36 g
- Fat: 34 g
- Carbohydrates: 14 g

Total time: 21 minutes

Preparation time: 10 minutes
Cooking time: 11 minutes
Servings: 4

Ingredients:
- ½ cup carrot, chopped
- 1 yellow onion, chopped
- 12 cups chicken stock
- 2 cups kale, chopped
- 3 cups chicken meat, cooked and shredded
- 1 cup orzo
- ¼ cup lemon juice
- 1 tablespoon olive oil

Directions:
1. Heat up a pot with the oil over medium heat, add the onion and sauté for 3 minutes.
2. Add the carrots and the rest of the ingredients, stir, bring to a simmer and cook for 8 minutes more.
3. Ladle into bowls and serve hot.

Nutrition:
- calories 300,
- fat 12.2,
- fiber 5.4,
- carbs 16.5,
- protein 12.2

Total time: 23 minutes

Preparation Time: 8 minutes
Cooking Time: 15 minutes
Servings: 4

Ingredients:
- Olive oil cooking spray
- 1-pound chicken tenders
- 1½ tablespoons zaatar
- ½ teaspoon kosher salt
- ¼ teaspoon freshly ground black pepper

Directions
1. In a large bowl, combine the chicken, zaatar, salt, and black pepper.
2. Mix together well, covering the chicken tenders fully.
3. Lay out in a single layer on the baking sheet and bake for 15 minutes, turning the chicken over once midway through the cooking time.

Nutrition:
- 304 calories
- 19g fats
- 7g protein

Total Time: 24 minutes

Preparation Time: 10 minutes
Cooking Time: 14 minutes
Servings: 4

Ingredients:
- 3 chicken breasts, skinless, boneless, and cut into chunks
- 1/4 fresh parsley, chopped
- 1 zucchini, sliced
- 2 bell peppers, chopped
- 1 cup rice, rinsed and drained
- 1 ½ cup chicken broth
- 1 tbsp oregano
- 3 tbsp fresh lemon juice
- 1 tbsp garlic, minced
- 1 onion, diced
- 2 tbsp olive oil
- Pepper
- Salt

Directions:
1. Add oil into the inner pot of instant pot and set the pot on sauté mode.
2. Add onion and chicken and cook for 5 minutes.
3. Add rice, oregano, lemon juice, garlic, broth, pepper, and salt and stir everything well.
4. Seal pot with lid and cook on high for 4 minutes.
5. Once done, release pressure using quick release.
6. Remove lid. Add parsley, zucchini, and bell peppers and stir well.
7. Seal pot again with lid and select manual and set timer for 5 minutes.
8. Release pressure using quick release.
9. Remove lid. Stir well and serve.

Nutrition:
- Calories: 500

- Fat: 16.5 g
- Carbohydrates: 48 g
- Protein: 38.7 g

Total Time: 25 minutes

Preparation Time: 5 minutes
Cooking Time: 20 minutes
Servings: 4

Ingredients:
- 2½ cups water
- ½ teaspoon kosher salt
- ¾ cups whole-grain cornmeal
- ¼ teaspoon freshly ground black pepper
- 2 tablespoons grated Parmesan cheese
- 1 tablespoon extra-virgin olive oil
- 1 bunch (about 6 ounces) Swiss chard, leaves and stems chopped and separated
- 2 garlic cloves, sliced
- ¼ teaspoon kosher salt
- 1/8 teaspoon freshly ground black pepper
- Lemon juice (optional)
- 1 tablespoon extra-virgin olive oil
- 4 large eggs

Directions:
1. For the polenta, bring the water and salt to a boil in a medium saucepan over high heat. Slowly add the cornmeal, whisking constantly.
2. Decrease the heat to low, cover, and cook for 10 to 15 minutes, stirring often to avoid lumps.
3. Stir in the pepper and Parmesan and divide among 4 bowls.
4. For the chard, heat the oil in a large skillet over medium heat.
5. Add the chard stems, garlic, salt, and pepper; sauté for 2 minutes.
6. Add the chard leaves and cook until wilted, about 3 to 5 minutes.
7. Add a spritz of lemon juice (if desired), toss together, and divide evenly on top of the polenta.
8. For the eggs, heat the oil in the same large skillet over medium-high heat.
9. Crack each egg into the skillet, taking care not to crowd the skillet and leaving space between the eggs.

10. Cook until the whites are set and golden around the edges, about 2 to 3 minutes.
11. Serve sunny-side up or flip the eggs over carefully and cook 1 minute longer for over easy.
12. Place one egg on top of the polenta and chard in each bowl.

Nutrition:
- Calories: 310
- Protein: 17 g
- Fat: 18 g
- Carbs: 21 g

TASTY BEEF AND BROCCOLI

Total time: 25 minutes

Preparation Time: 10 minutes
Cooking Time: 15 minutes
Servings: 4

Ingredients:
- 1 and ½ pounds flanks steak, cut into thin strips
- 1 tablespoon olive oil
- 1 tablespoon tamari sauce
- 1 cup beef stock
- 1-pound broccoli, florets separated

Directions:
1. In a bowl, mix steak strips with oil and tamari, toss and leave aside for 10 minutes.
2. Set your instant pot on sauté mode, add beef strips and brown them for 4 minutes on each side.
3. Add stock, stir, cover pot again and cook on high for 8 minutes.
4. Add broccoli, stir, cover pot again and cook on high for 4 minutes more.
5. Divide everything between plates and serve.
6. Enjoy!

Nutrition:
- Calories: 312
- Protein: 4 g
- Fat: 5 g
- Carbohydrates: 20 g

ROASTED BRUSSELS SPROUTS AND PECANS

Total time: 25 minutes

Preparation Time: 10 minutes
Cooking Time: 15 minutes
Servings: 4

Ingredients:
- 1 ½ lb. fresh Brussels sprouts
- 4 tbsp. olive oil 4 cloves of garlic, minced
- 3 tbsp. water Salt and pepper to taste
- ½ cup chopped pecans

Directions:
1. Place all ingredients in the Instant Pot.
2. Combine all ingredients until well combined.
3. Close the lid and make sure that the steam release vent is set to "Venting."
4. Press the "Slow Cook" button and adjust the cooking time to 3 hours.
5. Sprinkle with a dash of lemon juice if desired.

Nutrition:
- Calories: 161;
- Carbs: 10.2g;
- Protein: 4.1g;
- Fat: 13.1g

TUSCAN SOUP

Total time: 25 minutes

Preparation time: 10 minutes
Cooking time: 15 minutes
Servings: 6

Ingredients:
- 1 yellow onion, chopped
- 4 garlic cloves, minced
- 2 tablespoons olive oil
- ½ cup celery, chopped
- ½ cup carrots, chopped
- 15 ounces canned tomatoes, chopped
- 1 zucchini, chopped
- 6 cups veggie stock
- 2 tablespoons tomato paste
- 15 ounces canned white beans, drained and rinsed
- 2 handfuls baby spinach
- 1 tablespoon basil, chopped
- Salt and black pepper to the taste

Directions:
1. Heat up a pot with the oil over medium heat, add the garlic and the onion and sauté for 5 minutes.
2. Add the rest of the ingredients, stir, bring the soup to a simmer and cook for 10 minutes.
3. Ladle the soup into bowls and serve right away.

Nutrition:
- calories 471,
- fat 8.2,
- fiber 19.4,
- carbs 76.5,
- protein 27.6

CHEESY TOMATO LINGUINE

Total time: 26 minutes

Preparation time: 15 minutes
Cooking time: 11 minutes
Servings: 4

Ingredients:
- 2 tablespoons olive oil
- 1 small onion, diced
- 2 garlic cloves, minced
- 1 cup cherry tomatoes, halved
- 1½ cups vegetable stock
- ¼ cup julienned basil leaves
- 1 teaspoon salt
- ½ teaspoon ground black pepper
- ¼ teaspoon red chili flakes
- 1 pound (454 g) Linguine noodles, halved
- Fresh basil leaves for garnish
- ½ cup Parmigiano-Reggiano cheese, grated

Directions:
1. Warm oil on Sauté.
2. Add onion and Sauté for 2 minutes until soft.
3. Mix garlic and tomatoes and sauté for 4 minutes.
4. To the pot, add vegetable stock, salt, julienned basil, red chili flakes and pepper.
5. Add linguine to the tomato mixture until covered.
6. Seal the lid and cook on High Pressure for 5 minutes.
7. Naturally release the pressure for 5 minutes.
8. Stir the mixture to ensure it is broken down.
9. Divide into plates.
10. Top with basil and Parmigiano-Reggiano cheese and serve.

Nutrition:
- Calories: 311
- Fat: 11.3g
- Protein: 10.3g

- Carbs: 42.1g

SPAGHETTI WITH PINE NUTS AND CHEESE

Total time: 26 minutes

Preparation time: 15 minutes
Cooking time: 11 minutes
Servings: 4-6

Ingredients:
- 8 ounces (227 g) spaghetti
- 4 tablespoons almond butter
- 1 teaspoon freshly ground black pepper
- ½ cup pine nuts 1 cup fresh grated Parmesan cheese, divided

Directions:
1. Bring a large pot of salted water to a boil.
2. Add the pasta and cook for 8 minutes.
3. In a large saucepan over medium heat, combine the butter, black pepper, and pine nuts.
4. Cook for 2 to 3 minutes, or until the pine nuts are lightly toasted.
5. Reserve ½ cup of the pasta water.
6. Drain the pasta and place it into the pan with the pine nuts.
7. Add ¾ cup of the Parmesan cheese and the reserved pasta water to the pasta and toss everything together to evenly coat the pasta.
8. Transfer the pasta to a serving dish and top with the remaining ¼ cup of the Parmesan cheese.
9. Serve immediately.

Nutrition:
- Calories: 542
- Fat: 32.0g
- Protein: 20.0g
- Carbs: 46.0g

Total time: 30 minutes

Preparation time: 15 minutes
Cooking time: 15 minutes
Servings: 2

Ingredients:
- 1 cup chicken stock
- 1 cup frozen spinach, thawed
- 1 batch pasta dough

Filling:
- 3 tbsp heavy cream
- 1 cup ricotta
- 1 ¾ cups baby spinach
- 1 small onion, finely chopped
- 2 tbsp butter

Directions:

Create the filling:
1. In a fry pan, sauté onion and butter around five minutes.
2. Add the baby spinach leaves and continue simmering for another four minutes.
3. Remove from fire, drain liquid and mince the onion and leaves.
4. Then combine with 2 tbsp cream and the ricotta ensuring that it is well combined.
5. Add pepper and salt to taste.
6. With your pasta dough, divide it into four balls.
7. Roll out one ball to ¼ inch thick rectangular spread.
8. Cut a 1 ½ inch by 3-inch rectangles.
9. Place filling on the middle of the rectangles, around 1 tablespoonful and brush filling with cold water.
10. Fold the rectangles in half, ensuring that no air is trapped within and seal using a cookie cutter.
11. Use up all the filling.

Create Pasta Sauce:

1. Until smooth, puree chicken stock and spinach.
2. Pour into heated fry pan and for two minutes cook it.
3. Add 1 tbsp cream and season with pepper and salt.
4. Continue cooking for a minute and turn of fire.
5. Cook the raviolis by submerging in a boiling pot of water with salt.
6. Cook until al dente then drains.
7. Then quickly transfer the cooked ravioli into the fry pan of pasta sauce, toss to mix and serve.

Nutrition:
- Calories: 443
- Carbs: 12.3g
- Protein: 18.8g
- Fat: 36.8g

BEAN AND VEGGIE PASTA

Total time: 30 minutes

Preparation time: 15 minutes
Cooking time: 15 minutes
Servings: 4

Ingredients:
1. 16 ounces (454 g) small whole wheat pasta, such as penne, farfalle, or macaroni
2. 5 cups water
3. 1 (15-ounce / 425-g) can cannellini beans, drained and rinsed
4. 1 (14.5-ounce / 411-g) can diced (with juice) or crushed tomatoes
5. 1 yellow onion, chopped
6. 1 red or yellow bell pepper, chopped
7. 2 tablespoons tomato paste
8. 1 tablespoon olive oil
9. 3 garlic cloves, minced
10. ¼ teaspoon crushed red pepper (optional)
11. 1 bunch kale, stemmed and chopped
12. 1 cup sliced basil
13. ½ cup pitted Kalamata olives, chopped

Directions:
1. Add the pasta, water, beans, tomatoes (with juice if using diced), onion, bell pepper, tomato paste, oil, garlic, and crushed red pepper (if desired), to a large stockpot.
2. Bring to a boil over high heat, stirring often.
3. Reduce the heat to medium-high, add the kale, and cook, continuing to stir often, until the pasta is al dente, about 10 minutes.
4. Remove from the heat and let sit for 5 minutes.
5. Garnish with the basil and olives and serve.

Nutrition:
- Calories: 565
- Fat: 17.7g
- Protein: 18.0g
- Carbs: 85.5g

Total time: 30 minutes

Preparation time: 10 minutes
Cooking time: 20 minutes
Servings: 4

Ingredients:
- 1-pound Italian pork sausage, sliced
- ¼ cup olive oil
- 1 carrot, chopped
- 1 yellow onion, chopped
- 1 celery stalk, chopped
- 2 garlic cloves, minced
- ½ pound kale, chopped
- 4 cups chicken stock
- 28 ounces canned cannellini beans, drained and rinsed
- 1 bay leaf
- 1 teaspoon rosemary, dried
- Salt and black pepper to the taste
- ½ cup parmesan, grated

Directions:
1. Heat up a pot with the oil over medium heat, add the sausage and brown for 5 minutes.
2. Add the onion, carrots, garlic and celery and sauté for 3 minutes more.
3. Add the rest of the ingredients except the parmesan, bring to a simmer and cook over medium heat for 30 minutes.
4. Discard the bay leaf, ladle the soup into bowls, sprinkle the parmesan on top and serve.

Nutrition:
- calories 564,
- fat 26.5,
- fiber 15.4,
- carbs 37.4,
- protein 26.6

FISH SOUP

Total time: 30 minutes

Preparation time: 10 minutes
Cooking time: 20 minutes
Servings: 4

Ingredients:
- 2 tablespoons olive oil
- 1 tablespoon garlic, minced
- ½ cup tomatoes, crushed
- 1 yellow onion, chopped
- 1-quart veggie stock
- 1-pound cod, skinless, boneless and cubed
- ¼ teaspoon rosemary, dried
- A pinch of salt and black pepper

Directions:
1. Heat up a pot with the oil over medium heat, add the onion and the garlic and sauté for 5 minutes.
2. Add the rest of the ingredients, toss, simmer over medium heat for 15 minutes more, divide into bowls and serve for lunch.

Nutrition:
- calories 198,
- fat 8.1,
- fiber 1,
- carbs 4.2,
- protein 26.4

ZUCCHINI SOUP

Total time: 30 minutes

Preparation time: 10 minutes
Cooking time: 20 minutes
Servings: 8

Ingredients:
- 2 and ½ pounds zucchinis, roughly chopped
- 2 tablespoons olive oil
- 1 yellow onion, chopped
- 4 garlic cloves, minced
- 4 cups chicken stock
- ½ cup basil, chopped
- Salt and black pepper to the taste

Directions:
1. Heat up a pot with the oil over medium heat, add the zucchinis and the onion and sauté for 5 minutes.
2. Add the garlic and the rest of the ingredients except the basil, stir, bring to a simmer and cook for 15 minutes over medium heat.
3. Add the basil, blend the soup using an immersion blender, ladle into bowls and serve.

Nutrition:
- calories 182,
- fat 7.6,
- fiber 1.5,
- carbs 12.6,
- protein 2.3

SPICY SEAFOOD RISOTTO

Total Time: 30 minutes

Preparation time: 5 minutes
Cooking time: 15 minutes
Servings: 4

Ingredients:
- 3 cups of clam juice
- 2 cups of water
- 2 tablespoons of olive oil
- 1 medium-sized chopped up onion
- 2 minced cloves of garlic
- 1 ½ cups of Arborio Rice
- ½ cup of dry white wine
- 1 teaspoon of Saffron
- ½ teaspoon of ground cumin
- ½ teaspoon of paprika
- 1 pound of marinara seafood mix
- Salt as needed
- Ground pepper as needed

Directions:
1. Place a saucepan over high heat and pour in your clam juice with water and bring the mixture to a boil. Remove the heat.
2. Take a heavy bottomed saucepan and stir fry your garlic and onion in oil over medium heat until a nice fragrance comes off.
3. Add in the rice and keep stirring for 2-3 minutes until the rice has been fully covered with the oil. Pour the wine and then add the saffron.
4. Keep stirring constantly until it is fully absorbed.
5. Add in the cumin, clam juice, paprika mixture 1 cup at a time, making sure to keep stirring it from time to time.
6. Cook the rice for 20 minutes until perfect.
7. Add the seafood marinara mix and cook for another 5-7 minutes.
8. Season with some pepper and salt.
9. Transfer the meal to a serving dish. Serve hot.

Nutrition:

- Calories: 386
- Fat: 7g
- Carbohydrates: 55g
- Protein: 21g 82.

PARMESAN-SAUTÉED ZUCCHINI WITH SPAGHETTI

Total time: 30 minutes

Preparation time: 15 minutes
Cooking time: 15 minutes
Servings: 4

Ingredients:
- 8 ounces dry whole-grain spaghetti
- 2 tablespoons olive oil
- 1 tablespoon minced garlic
- 4 zucchinis, chopped
- ½ cup grated Parmesan cheese, divided
- Sea salt
- Freshly ground black pepper

Directions:
1. Bring a large pot of water to a boil and cook the pasta according to the package instructions until al dente. Drain.
2. While the pasta is cooking, in a large skillet, heat the olive oil over medium-high heat.
3. Sauté the garlic until softened, about 2 minutes.
4. Add the zucchini and sauté until the squash is lightly caramelized, about 5 minutes.
5. Stir in ¼ cup of Parmesan cheese and toss until the cheese is melted and lightly browned. Add the cooked spaghetti to the skillet and toss to coat.
6. Season with salt and pepper
7. Serve topped with the remaining ¼ cup of Parmesan cheese.

Nutrition:
- Calories: 338
- Fat: 11g
- Carbohydrates: 50g
- Protein: 15g

BRAISED SHORT RIBS WITH RED WINE

Total time: 12 minutes

Preparation Time: 10 minutes
Cooking Time: 2 minutes
Servings: 4

Ingredients:
- 1½ pounds boneless beef short ribs (if using bone-in, use 3½ pounds)
- 1 teaspoon salt ½ teaspoon freshly ground black pepper
- ½ teaspoon garlic powder
- ¼ cup extra-virgin olive oil
- 1 cup dry red wine (such as cabernet sauvignon or merlot)
- 2 to 3 cups beef broth, divided
- 4 sprigs rosemary

Directions:
1. Preheat the oven to 350°F.
2. Season the short ribs with salt, pepper, and garlic powder.
3. Let sit for 10 minutes.
4. In a Dutch oven or oven-safe deep skillet, heat the olive oil over medium-high heat.
5. When the oil is very hot, add the short ribs and brown until dark in color, 2 to 3 minutes per side.
6. Remove the meat from the oil and keep warm.
7. Add the red wine and 2 cups beef broth to the Dutch oven, whisk together, and bring to a boil.
8. Reduce the heat to low and simmer until the liquid is reduced to about 2 cups, about 10 minutes.
9. Return the short ribs to the liquid, which should come about halfway up the meat, adding up to 1 cup of remaining broth if needed.
10. Cover and braise until the meat are very tender, about 1½ to 2 hours.
11. Remove from the oven and let sit, covered, for 10 minutes before serving.
12. Serve warm, drizzled with cooking liquid.

Nutrition:
- Calories: 792
- Total Fat: 76g
- Total Carbs: 2g
- Net Carbs: 2g
- Fiber: 0g
- Protein: 25g   Sodium: 783mg

CHICKEN PIZZA

Total time: 15 minutes

Preparation Time: 5 minutes
Cooking Time: 10 minutes
Servings: 4

Ingredients:
- 2 flatbreads
- 1 tbsp. Greek vinaigrette
- ½ cup feta cheese, crumbled
- ¼ cup Parmesan cheese, grated
- ½ cup water-packed artichoke hearts, rinsed, drained and chopped
- ½ cup olives, pitted and sliced
- ½ cup cooked chicken breast strips, chopped
- 1/8 tsp. dried basil
- 1/8 tsp. dried oregano
- Pinch of ground black pepper
- 1 cup part-skim mozzarella cheese, shredded

Directions:
1. Preheat the oven to 400°F.
2. Arrange the flatbreads onto a large ungreased baking sheet and coat each with vinaigrette.
3. Top with feta, followed by the Parmesan, veggies and chicken. Sprinkle with dried herbs and black pepper.
4. Top with mozzarella cheese evenly.
5. Bake for about 8-10 minutes or until cheese is melted.
6. Remove from the oven and set aside for about 1-2 minutes before slicing.
7. Cut each flat bread into 2 pieces and serve.

Nutrition:
- Calories 393
- Fat 22 g
- Carbs 20.6 g
- Protein 28.9

Total time: 18 minutes

Preparation Time: 10 minutes
Cooking Time: 8 minutes
Serving: 8

Ingredients:
- 8 trimmed lamb loin chops
- 2 tbsp lemon juice
- 1 tbsp dried oregano
- 1 tbsp minced garlic
- ½ tsp salt
- ¼ tsp black pepper

Direction:
1. Preheat the broiler Combine oregano, garlic, lemon juice, salt and pepper and rub on both sides of the lamb.
2. Situate lamb on a broiler pan coated with cooking spray and cook for 4 min on each side.

Nutrition:
- 457 Calories
- 49g Protein
- 20g Fat

CURRY SALMON WITH MUSTARD

Total time: 18 minutes

Preparation Time: 10 minutes
Cooking Time: 8 minutes
Servings: 4

Ingredients:
- ¼ tsp. ground red pepper or chili powder
- ¼ tsp. ground turmeric
- ¼ tsp. salt
- 1 tsp. honey
- 1/8 tsp. garlic powder or 1 clove garlic minced
- 2 teaspoons. whole grain mustard
- 4 pcs 6-oz salmon fillets

Directions:
1. In a small bowl mix well salt, garlic powder, red pepper, turmeric, honey and mustard.
2. Preheat oven to broil and grease a baking dish with cooking spray.
3. Place salmon on baking dish with skin side down and spread evenly mustard mixture on top of salmon.
4. Pop in the oven and broil until flaky around 8 minutes.

Nutrition:
- Calories: 324;
- Fat: 18.9 g;
- Protein: 34 g;
- Carbs: 2.9 g

SAGANAKI SHRIMP

Total time: 20 minutes

Preparation Time: 10 minutes
Cooking Time: 10 minutes
Servings: 4

Ingredients:
- ¼ tsp. salt
- ½ cup Chardonnay
- ½ cup crumbled Greek feta cheese
- 1 medium bulb. fennel, cored and finely chopped
- 1 small Chile pepper, seeded and minced
- 1 tbsp. extra virgin olive oil
- 12 jumbo shrimps, peeled and deveined with tails left on
- 2 tbsp. lemon juice, divided
- 5 scallions sliced thinly Pepper to Taste

Directions:
1. In medium bowl, mix salt, lemon juice and shrimp.
2. On medium fire, place a saganaki pan (or large nonstick saucepan) and heat oil. Sauté Chile pepper, scallions, and fennel for 4 minutes or until starting to brown and is already soft.
3. Add wine and sauté for another minute.
4. Place shrimps on top of fennel, cover and cook for 4 minutes or until shrimps are pink.
5. Remove just the shrimp and transfer to a plate.
6. Add pepper, feta and 1 tbsp. lemon juice to pan and cook for a minute or until cheese begins to melt.
7. To serve, place cheese and fennel mixture on a serving plate and top with shrimps.

Nutrition:
- Calories: 310;
- Protein: 49.7g;
- Fat: 6.8g;
- Carbs: 8.4g

Total time: 20 minutes

Preparation Time: 5 minutes
Cooking Time: 15 minutes
Servings: 4

Ingredients:

- 1 ½ lb. steak mince
- 2/3 cup beef stock
- 3 oz. Mozzarella or cheddar cheese, grated
- 3 oz. butter, melted
- 7 oz. breadcrumbs
- 1 tablespoon extra-virgin olive oil
- 1 x roast vegetable pack
- 1 x red onion, diced
- 1 x red pepper, diced
- 1 x 14 oz. can chop tomatoes
- 1 x zucchini, diced
- 3 cloves garlic, crushed
- 1 tablespoon Worcestershire sauce

For the topping...

- Fresh thyme

Directions:

1. Pop a skillet over a medium heat and add the oil.
2. Add the red pepper, onion, zucchini and garlic.
3. Cook for 5 minutes.
4. Add the beef and cook for five minutes.
5. Throw in the tinned tomatoes, beef stock and Worcestershire sauce then stir well.
6. Bring to the boil then simmer for 6 minutes.
7. Divide between the bowls and top with the thyme.
8. Serve and enjoy.

Nutrition:

- Calories: 678

- Net carbs: 24g
- Fat: 45g
- Protein: 48g

Total time: 21 minutes

Preparation Time: 15 minutes
Cooking Time: 6 minutes
Serving: 4

Ingredients:
- 1-pound chicken breast
- 4 (6-inch) halved pitas
- ½ cup chopped plum tomato
- ½ cup chopped cucumber
- ¼ cup chopped red onion
- 5 tbsp plain low-fat Greek-style yogurt, divided
- 2 tbsp lemon juice, divided
- 2 tbsp finely chopped parsley
- 2 tbsp extra-virgin olive oil
- 1 tbsp tahini
- ½ tsp salt
- ½ tsp crushed red pepper
- ¼ tsp ground cumin
- ¼ tsp ground ginger
- 1/8 tsp ground coriander

Direction:
1. Combine the parsley, salt, red pepper, ginger, cumin, coriander, 1 tbsp of yogurt, 1 tbsp of juice and 2 cloves of garlic.
2. Add the chicken, stir to coat.
3. Prep oil in nonstick pan over medium-high heat.
4. Add the chicken mixture to the pan and cook for 6 min Scourge remaining 1 tbsp of lemon juice, the remaining ¼ cup of yogurt, remaining 1 clove of garlic and the tahini, mixing well.
5. Put 1 ½ tsp of the tahini mixture inside each half of the pita, divide the chicken between the halves of the pita.
6. Fill each half of the pita with 1 tbsp of cucumber, 1 tbsp of tomato and 1 ½ tsp of onion.

Nutrition:

- 440 Calories
- 37g Protein
- 19g Fat

LEMON CHICKEN PITA BURGERS WITH SPICED YOGURT SAUCE

Total time: 21 minutes

Preparation Time: 15 minutes
Cooking Time: 6 minutes
Serving: 4

Ingredients:
- 4 (6-inch) cut in half pitas
- 2 lightly beaten large egg whites
- 1-pound ground chicken
- 2 cups shredded lettuce
- ½ cup diced tomato
- ½ cup chopped green onions
- ½ cup plain low-fat yogurt
- 1/3 cup Italian-seasoned breadcrumbs
- 1 tbsp olive oil
- 1 tbsp Greek seasoning blend
- 2 tsp grated lemon zest, divided
- 1 ½ tsp chopped oregano
- ½ tsp coarsely ground black pepper

Direction:
1. Combine the chicken, eggs, onion, black pepper, breadcrumbs, Greek seasoning blend and 1 tsp of zest, mixing well.
2. Split mixture into 8 equal portions and make patties ¼-inch thick.
3. Heat the oil in a large nonstick pan over medium-high heat.
4. Put on the patties and cook for 2 min per side.
5. Cover, lower the heat to medium and cook for 4 min.
6. Combine oregano, yogurt and the remaining zest.
7. Fill each half of the pita with 1 patty, 1 tbsp of yogurt mix, 1 tbsp of tomato and ¼ cup of lettuce.

Nutrition:
- 391 Calories
- 40g Protein
- 20g Fat

SHRIMP PIZZA

Total Time: 25 minutes

Preparation Time: 15 minutes
Cooking Time: 10 minutes
Servings: 1

Ingredients:
- 2 tbsp. spaghetti sauce
- 1 tbsp. pesto sauce
- 1 (6-inch) pita bread
- 2 tbsp. mozzarella cheese, shredded
- 5 cherry tomatoes, halved
- 1/8 cup bay shrimp
- Pinch of garlic powder
- Pinch of dried basil

Directions:
1. Preheat the oven to 325°F.
2. Lightly, grease a baking sheet.
3. In a bowl, mix together the spaghetti sauce and pesto.
4. Spread the pesto mixture over the pita bread in a thin layer.
5. Top the pita bread with the cheese, followed by the tomatoes and shrimp. Sprinkle with the garlic powder and basil.
6. Arrange the pita bread onto the prepared baking sheet and bake for about 7-10 minutes. Remove from the oven and set aside for about 3-5 minutes before slicing.
7. Cut into desired sized slices and serve.

Nutrition:
- Calories 482
- Fat 18.9 g
- Carbs 44.5 g
- Protein 33.4 g

Total time: 25 minutes

Preparation Time: 10 minutes
Cooking Time: 15 minutes
Servings: 4

Ingredients:
- 1 lb. ground beef
- 1/2 cup minced onions
- 1 tablespoon olive oil
- 1/2 teaspoon salt
- 1/2 teaspoon ground coriander
- 1/2 teaspoon ground cumin
- 1/4 teaspoon ground cinnamon
- 1/4 teaspoon allspice
- 1/4 teaspoon dried mint leaves

Directions:
1. Grab a large bowl and add all the ingredients.
2. Stir well to combine then use your hands to shape into ovals or balls.
3. Carefully thread onto skewers then brush with oil.
4. Pop into the grill and cook uncovered for 15 minutes, turning often.
5. Serve and enjoy.

Nutrition:
- Calories: 216
- Net carbs: 4g
- Fat: 19g
- Protein: 25g

BULGUR LAMB MEATBALLS

Total time: 25 minutes

Preparation Time: 10 minutes
Cooking Time: 15 minutes
Servings: 6

Ingredients:
- 1 and ½ cups Greek yogurt
- ½ teaspoon cumin, ground
- 1 cup cucumber, shredded
- ½ teaspoon garlic, minced
- A pinch of salt and black pepper
- 1 cup bulgur
- 2 cups water
- 1-pound lamb, ground
- ¼ cup parsley, chopped
- ¼ cup shallots, chopped
- ½ teaspoon allspice, ground
- ½ teaspoon cinnamon powder
- 1 tablespoon olive oil

Directions:
1. Mix the bulgur with the water, cover the bowl, leave aside for 10 minutes, drain and transfer to a bowl.
2. Add the meat, the yogurt and the rest of the ingredients except the oil, stir well and shape medium meatballs out of this mix.
3. Preheat pan over medium-high heat, place the meatballs, cook them for 7 minutes on each side, arrange them all on a platter and serve as an appetizer.

Nutrition:
- Calories 300
- Fat 9.6g
- Carbohydrates 22.6g
- Protein 6.6g

CAJUN GARLIC SHRIMP NOODLE BOWL

Total time: 25 minutes

Preparation Time: 10 minutes
Cooking Time: 15 minutes
Servings: 2

Ingredients:
- ½ tsp. salt
- 1 onion, sliced
- 1 red pepper, sliced
- 1 tbsp. butter
- 1 tsp. garlic granules
- 1 tsp. onion powder
- 1 tsp. paprika
- 2 large zucchinis, cut into noodle strips
- 20 jumbo shrimps, shells removed and deveined
- 3 cloves garlic, minced
- 3 tbsp. ghee A dash of cayenne pepper
- A dash of red pepper flakes

Directions:
1. Prepare the Cajun seasoning by mixing the onion powder, garlic granules, pepper flakes, cayenne pepper, paprika and salt.
2. Toss in the shrimp to coat in the seasoning.
3. In a skillet, heat the ghee and sauté the garlic. Add in the red pepper and onions and continue sautéing for 4 minutes.
4. Add the Cajun shrimp and cook until opaque. Set aside.
5. In another pan, heat the butter and sauté the zucchini noodles for three minutes. Assemble by the placing the Cajun shrimps on top of the zucchini noodles.

Nutrition:
- Calories: 712;
- Fat: 30.0g;
- Protein: 97.8g;
- Carbs: 20.2g

Total Time: 25 minutes

Preparation Time: 5 minutes
Cooking Time: 20 minutes
Servings: 4

Ingredients:
- 1/8 teaspoons black pepper, add as per taste
- 1/3 cup of Extra virgin olive oil
- 4 lightly beaten eggs
- 7 cups of Lettuce, preferably a spring mix (mesclun)
- 1/2 cup of crumbled Feta cheese
- 1/8 teaspoon of Sea salt, add to taste
- 1 finely chopped medium
- Yellow onion

Directions:
1. Warm the oven to 180C and grease the flan dish.
2. Once done, pour the extra virgin olive oil into a large saucepan and heat it over medium heat with the onions, until they are translucent.
3. Add greens and keep stirring until all the ingredients are wilted.
4. Season it with salt and pepper and transfer the greens to the prepared dish and sprinkle on some feta cheese.
5. Pour the eggs and bake it for 20 minutes till it is cooked through and slightly brown.

Nutrition:
- Calories: 325
- Protein: 11.2 g
- Fat: 27.9 g
- Carbs: 7.3 g

LOW-CARB BAKED EGGS WITH AVOCADO AND FETA

Total Time: 25 minutes

Preparation Time: 10 minutes
Cooking Time: 15 minutes
Servings: 2

Ingredients:
- 1 avocado
- 4 eggs
- 2-3 tbsp. crumbled feta cheese
- Nonstick cooking spray
- Pepper and salt to taste

Directions:
1. First, you will have to preheat the oven to 400 degrees f.
2. After that, when the oven is on the proper temperature, you will have to put the gratin dishes right on the baking sheet.
3. Then, leave the dishes to heat in the oven for almost 10 minutes
4. After that process, you need to break the eggs into individual ramekins.
5. Then, let the avocado and eggs come to room temperature for at least 10 minutes.
6. Then, peel the avocado properly and cut it each half into 6-8 slices.
7. You will have to remove the dishes from the oven and spray them with the non-stick spray.
8. Then, you will have to arrange all the sliced avocados in the dishes and tip two eggs into each dish.
9. Sprinkle with feta, add pepper and salt to taste.
10. Serve.

Nutrition:
- Calories: 280
- Protein: 11 g
- Fat: 23 g
- Carbs: 10 g

Total Time: 25 minutes

Preparation Time: 20 minutes
Cooking Time: 5 minutes
Servings: 6

Ingredients:
- 1 cup mozzarella cheese, shredded
- 2/3 cup ricotta cheese
- 2 tsp. avocado oil
- 1 large whole-wheat pizza crust
- ¼ cup basil, chopped
- 1 ½ cups broccoli florets, chopped
- ½ tsp. garlic powder
- Cornmeal (for dusting)
- 1 ½ cups corn kernels
- Ground black pepper and salt, to taste

Directions:
1. Preheat your oven at 400°F.
2. Take a baking sheet, line it with parchment paper.
3. Grease it with some avocado oil.
4. Spread some cornmeal over the baking sheet In a mixing bowl, combine the corn, broccoli, ricotta, mozzarella, scallions, garlic powder, basil, black pepper and salt.
5. Place the pizza crust on the baking sheet.
6. Add the topping mixture on top and bake until the top is light brown, for 12-15 minutes.
7. Slice and serve warm!

Nutrition:
- Calories: 417
- Fat: 11g
- Carbs: 53g
- Protein 19g

Total Time: 25 minutes

Preparation Time: 10 minutes
Cooking Time: 15 minutes
Servings: 6

Ingredients:
- 2 tbsp. cornmeal
- 1 cup mozzarella
- 1/3 cup barbecue sauce
- 1 roma tomato, diced
- 1 cup black beans
- 1 cup corn kernels
- 1 medium whole-wheat pizza crust

Directions:
1. Preheat your oven at 400°F.
2. Take a baking sheet, line it with parchment paper.
3. Grease it with some avocado oil.
4. Spread some cornmeal over the baking sheet.
5. In a bowl, mix together the tomatoes, corn and beans.
6. Place the pizza crust on the baking sheet.
7. Spread the sauce on top; add the topping, and top with the cheese and bake until the cheese melts and the crust edges are golden-brown for 12-15 minutes.
8. Slice and serve warm.

Nutrition:
- Calories: 223
- Fat: 14g
- Carbs: 41g
- Protein: 8g

GREEK TURKEY BURGERS

Total time: 25 minutes

Preparation Time: 15 minutes
Cooking Time: 10 minutes
Serving: 4

Ingredients:
- 4 Whole-Wheat hamburger buns
- 1 pound 93% lean ground turkey
- 2 cups arugula
- ½ cup sliced cucumber
- ½ cup thinly sliced red onion
- 1/3 cup chopped kalamata olives
- 1/3 cup plain whole-milk Greek yogurt
- ¼ cup canola mayonnaise
- 1 tbsp lemon juice
- 2 tsp dried oregano
- 1 tsp ground cumin
- ¼ tsp kosher salt
- ¼ tsp black pepper, divided

Direction:
1. Combine turkey, oregano, cumin, mayonnaise, salt and 1/8 tsp of pepper.
2. Form the mixture into 4 patties.
3. Heat a big cast-iron pan at high heat.
4. Slightly coat the pan with cooking spray and add the turkey patties.
5. Cook for about 4 to 5 min per side.
6. Combine the yogurt, lemon juice, olives and the remaining 1/8 tsp of pepper in a small bowl.
7. Sprinkle the yogurt mixture on the cut sides of the top and bottom buns.
8. Divide the arugula between the lower halves of the sandwiches, garnish with cooked patties, cucumber and red onion.
9. Wrap with the top halves of the rolls and serve.

Nutrition:
- 459 Calories

- 48g Protein
- 19g Fat

Total time: 30 minutes

Preparation Time: 20 minutes
Cooking Time: 10 minutes
Servings: 6-8

Ingredients:
For the beef skewer
- 1 ½ lb. skirt steak, cut into cubes
- 1 teaspoon grated lemon zest
- ½ teaspoon coriander seeds, ground
- ½ teaspoon salt
- 2 garlic cloves, chopped
- 2 tablespoons olive oil
- 2 bell peppers, seeded and cubed
- 4 small green zucchinis, cubed
- 24 cherry tomatoes
- 2 tablespoons extra virgin olive oil

To serve...
Store-bought hummus 1 lemon, cut into wedges

Directions:
1. Grab a large bowl and add all the ingredients.
2. Stir well. Cover and pop into the fridge for at least 30 minutes, preferably overnight.
3. Preheat the grill to high and oil the grate.
4. Take a medium bowl and add the peppers, zucchini, tomatoes and oil.
5. Season well Just before cooking, start threading everything onto the skewers.
6. Alternate veggies and meat as you wish.
7. Pop into the grill and cook for 5 minutes on each side.
8. Serve and enjoy.

Nutrition:
- Calories: 938
- Net carbs: 65g
- Fat: 25g
- Protein: 87g

Total time:30 minutes

Preparation Time: 10 minutes
Cooking Time: 20 minutes
Servings: 6

Ingredients:
- 1-1/2 lb. pork tenderloin
- 1 teaspoon coarsely ground pepper
- 2 tablespoons extra virgin olive oil
- 3 quarts water
- 1 1/4 cups uncooked orzo pasta
- 1/4 teaspoon salt
- 6 oz. fresh baby spinach
- 1 cup grape tomatoes, halved
- 3/4 cup crumbled feta cheese

Directions:
1. Place the pork onto a flat surface and rub with the pepper.
2. Cut into the 1" cubes.
3. Place a skillet over a medium heat and add the oil.
4. Add the pork and cook for 10 minutes until no longer pink.
5. Fill a Dutch oven with water and place over a medium heat.
6. Bring to a boil. Stir in the orzo and cook uncovered for 8-10 minutes.
7. Stir through the spinach then drain.
8. Add the tomatoes to the pork, heat through then stir through orzo and cheese.
9. Serve and enjoy.

Nutrition:
- Calories: 372
- Net carbs: 34g
- Fat: 11g
- Protein: 31g

GRILLED PORK CHOPS WITH TOMATO SALAD

Total time: 30 minutes

Preparation Time: 15 minutes
Cooking Time: 15 minutes
Servings: 4

Ingredients:
For the pork chops...
- 4 x 6 oz. boneless pork chops
- 1 tablespoon canola oil
- 1-2 tablespoons dry rub pork seasoning
- 1 teaspoon dried oregano

For the tomato salad...
- 1 lb. medium size tomatoes, quartered
- 1 cup fresh Italian flat leaf parsley, leaves roughly chopped
- 1/3 cup sliced red onion
- 1/4 cup capers
- 1 clove garlic, pressed or minced
- 2 tablespoons extra virgin olive oil
- 1/2 lemon
- 1/2 teaspoon kosher salt
- 1/2 teaspoon freshly ground black pepper
- 1/2 cup feta cheese

Directions:
1. Preheat the grill to 350°F.
2. Brush the pork chops with oil and season well with the rub and oregano.
3. Leave to rest for 5-10 minutes as the grill warms.
4. Meanwhile, grab a large bowl and add the salad ingredients.
5. Stir well and pop into the fridge until ready to be served.
6. Cook the pork chops for 10 minutes or so, turning halfway through.
7. Remove from the pan and leave to rest for five minutes before cutting.
8. Enjoy with the salad and chunks of feta.

Nutrition:
- Calories: 340

- Net carbs: 6g
- Fat: 20g
- Protein: 31g

FLANK STEAK WITH ORANGE-HERB PISTOU

Total time: 30 minutes

Preparation Time: 10 minutes
Cooking Time: 20 minutes
Servings: 4

Ingredients:
- 1-pound flank steak
- 8 tablespoons extra-virgin olive oil, divided
- 2 teaspoons salt, divided
- 1 teaspoon freshly ground black pepper, divided
- ½ cup chopped fresh flat-leaf Italian parsley
- ¼ cup chopped fresh mint leaves
- 2 garlic cloves, roughly chopped Zest and juice of 1 orange or 2 clementines
- 1 teaspoon red pepper flakes (optional)
- 1 tablespoon red wine vinegar

Directions:
1. Heat the grill to medium-high heat or, if using an oven, preheat to 400°F.
2. Rub the steak with 2 tablespoons olive oil and sprinkle with 1 teaspoon salt and ½ teaspoon pepper.
3. Let sit at room temperature while you make the pistou.
4. In a food processor, combine the parsley, mint, garlic, orange zest and juice, remaining 1 teaspoon salt, red pepper flakes (if using), and remaining ½ teaspoon pepper.
5. Pulse until finely chopped.
6. With the processor running, stream in the red wine vinegar and remaining 6 tablespoons olive oil until well combined.
7. This pistou will be more oil-based than traditional basil pesto.
8. Cook the steak on the grill, 6 to 8 minutes per side.
9. Remove from the grill and allow to rest for 10 minutes on a cutting board.
10. If cooking in the oven, heat a large oven-safe skillet (cast iron works great) over high heat.
11. Add the steak and seer, 1 to 2 minutes per side, until browned.
12. Transfer the skillet to the oven and cook 10 to 12 minutes, or until the steak reaches your desired temperature.

13. To serve, slice the steak and drizzle with the pistou.

Nutrition:
- Calories: 441
- Total Fat: 36g
- Total Carbs: 3g
- Net Carbs: 3g
- Fiber: 0g
- Protein: 25g
- Sodium: 1237mg

EASY PORK CHOPS

Total time: 30 minutes

Preparation Time: 10 minutes
Cooking Time: 20 or so minutes
Servings: 4

Ingredients:
- 4 pork chops, boneless
- 1 tablespoon extra-virgin olive oil
- 1 cup chicken stock, low-sodium
- A pinch of black pepper
- 1 teaspoon sweet paprika

Directions:
1. Heat up a pan while using the oil over medium-high heat, add pork chops, brown them for 5 minutes on either side, add paprika, black pepper and stock, toss, cook for fifteen minutes more, divide between plates and serve by using a side salad.
2. Enjoy!

Nutrition:
- Calories: 272
- Fat: 4
- Fiber: 8
- Carbs: 14
- Protein: 17

BUTTERED PORK CHOPS

Total time: 30 minutes

Preparation Time: 15 minutes
Cooking Time: 15 minutes
Servings: 4

Ingredients:
- Pork Chops (4)
- Salt (1 t.)
- Bacon Grease (2 T.)
- Butter (4 T.)
- Pepper (1 t.)

Directions:
1. If you are looking for a quick and easy meal, look no further than buttered pork chops!
2. Within twenty minutes, you'll be sitting down and enjoying your meal.
3. You will want to start off this recipe by taking out your pork chops and seasoning them on either side.
4. If you need more than a teaspoon of salt and pepper, feel free to season as desired.
5. Next, you are going to want to place your skillet over high heat and place the bacon grease and butter into the bottom.
6. Once the butter is melted and the grease is sizzling, pop the pork chops into the skillet and sear on either side for three to four minutes.
7. In the end, the pork should be a nice golden color.
8. When the meat is cooked as desired, remove the skillet from the heat and enjoy your meal!

Nutrition:
- Calories: 450
- Fats: 30g
- Proteins: 45g

PORK CHOPS AND TOMATO SAUCE:

Total time: 30 minutes

Preparation Time: 10 minutes
Cooking Time: 20 minutes
Servings: 4

Ingredients:
- 4 pork chops, boneless
- 1 tablespoon soy sauce
- ¼ teaspoon sesame oil
- 1 and ½ cups tomato paste
- 1 yellow onion
- 8 mushrooms, sliced

Directions:
1. In a bowl, mix pork chops with soy sauce and sesame oil, toss and leave aside for 10 minutes.
2. Set your instant pot on sauté mode, add pork chops and brown them for 5 minutes on each side.
3. Add onion, stir and cook for 1-2 minutes more.
4. Add tomato paste and mushrooms, toss, cover and cook on high for 8-9 minutes.
5. Divide everything between plates and serve.
6. Enjoy!

Nutrition:
- Calories: 300
- Protein: 4 g
- Fat: 7 g
- Carbohydrates: 18 g

Total Time: 30 minutes

Preparation Time: 10 minutes
Cooking Time: 20 minutes
Servings: 8

Ingredients:
- 1 cup spinach, finely diced
- 1/2 yellow onion, finely diced
- 1/2 cup sliced sun-dried tomatoes
- 4 large basil leaves, finely diced
- Pepper and salt to taste
- 1/3 cup feta cheese crumbles
- 8 large eggs
- 1/4 cup milk (any kind)

Directions:
13. Warm the oven to 375°F.
14. Then, roll the dough sheet into a 12x8-inch rectangle.
15. Then, cut in half lengthwise.
16. After that, you will have to cut each half crosswise into 4 pieces, forming 8 (4x3-inch) pieces dough.
17. Then, press each into the bottom and up sides of the ungreased muffin cup.
18. Trim dough to keep the dough from touching, if essential. Set aside.
19. Then, you will have to combine the eggs, salt, pepper in the bowl and beat it with a whisk until well mixed. Set aside.
20. Melt the butter in 12-inch skillet over medium heat until sizzling; add bell peppers.
21. You will have to cook it, stirring occasionally, 2-3 minutes or until crisply tender.
22. After that, add spinach leaves; continue cooking until spinach is wilted. Then just add egg mixture and prosciutto.
23. Divide the mixture evenly among prepared muffin cups.
24. Bake it for 14-17 minutes or until the crust is golden brown.

Nutrition:
- Calories: 240
- Protein: 9 g

- Fat: 16 g
- Carbs: 13 g

Total Time: 30 minutes

Preparation Time: 18 minutes
 Cooking Time: 12 minutes
Servings: 6

Ingredients:
- 1 (12-inch) prepared pizza crust
- ¼ tsp. Italian seasoning
- ¼ tsp. red pepper flakes, crushed 1
- cup goat cheese, crumbled
- 1 (14-oz.) can quartered artichoke hearts
- 3 plum tomatoes, sliced into
- ¼-inch thick size
- 6 kalamata olives, pitted and sliced
- ¼ cup fresh basil, chopped

Directions:
1. Preheat the oven to 450°F.
2. Grease a baking sheet.
3. Sprinkle the pizza crust with Italian seasoning and red pepper flakes evenly.
4. Place the goat cheese over crust evenly, leaving about ½-inch of the sides.
5. With the back of a spoon, gently press the cheese downwards.
6. Place the artichoke, tomato and olives on top of the cheese.
7. Arrange the pizza crust onto the prepared baking sheet.
8. Bake for about 10-12 minutes or till cheese becomes bubbly.
9. Remove from oven and sprinkle with the basil.
10. Cut into equal sized wedges and serve.

Nutrition:
- Calories: 381
- Fat: 16.1 g
- Carbs: 42.4 g
- Protein: 19.4 g

Total Time: 30 minutes

Preparation time: 15 minutes
Cooking time: 12-15 minutes
Servings: 1

Ingredients: 1

- small (4 inches) pita bread
- 1/4 cup pizza sauce
- 4 slices cooked ham
- 1/4 cup pineapple chunks, drained
- 4 slices Monterey Jack cheese

Directions:

1. Preheat the oven to 250 degrees (400 degrees F).
2. Place the pita bread on a small baking sheet.
3. Cover with pizza sauce, ham, and pieces of pineapple garnish with Monterey Jack cheese.
4. Bake in the preheated oven for 12 to 15 minutes, until cheese is melted and light brown.

Nutrition:

- Calories: 276
- Carbs: 31g
- Fat: 11g
- Protein: 12g

SPROUTS PIZZA

Total Time: 30 minutes

Preparation time: 15 minutes
Cooking time: 15 minutes
Servings: 6

Ingredients:
- 4 oz wheat flour, whole grain
- 2 tablespoons olive oil
- ¼ teaspoon baking powder
- 5 oz chicken fillet, boiled
- 2 oz Mozzarella cheese, shredded
- 1 tomato, chopped 2 oz bean sprouts

Directions:
1. Make the pizza crust: mix wheat flour, olive oil, baking powder, and knead the dough.
2. Roll it up in the shape of pizza crust and transfer in the pizza mold.
3. Then sprinkle it with chopped tomato, shredded chicken, and Mozzarella.
4. Bake the pizza at 365F for 15 minutes.
5. Sprinkle the cooked pizza with bean sprouts and cut into servings.

Nutrition:
- Calories; 184
- Protein: 11.9g
- Carbohydrates: 15.6g
- Fat: 8.2g

SALTED PISTACHIO AND TAHINI TRUFFLES

Total Time: 5 minutes

Preparation Time: 5 minutes
Cooking Time: 0 minutes
Servings: 2

Ingredients
- 1/2 cup pure agave syrup
- 1/2 cup dates, pitted and soaked
- 1/3 cup tahini
- 1/3 cup shelled pistachios, roasted and salted
- 1 teaspoon pure vanilla extract
- 1/2 teaspoon ground cinnamon
- A pinch of sea salt
- 2 tablespoons carob powder
- 2 tablespoons cocoa powder
- 2 cups rolled oats

Directions
1. In your food processor, mix all of the above ingredients, except for the oats, until well combined.
2. Add in the rolled oats and stir with a wooden spoon.
3. Roll the mixture into small balls and place in your refrigerator until ready to serve.
4. Enjoy!

Nutrition:
- Calories: 224
- Fat: 9.5g
- Carbs: 38.7g
- Protein: 7.4g

Total Time: 5 minutes

Preparation Time: 5 minutes
Cooking Time: 0 minutes
Servings: 2

Ingredients:
- 2 bananas, peeled
- 1 cup unsweetened almond milk, or skim milk
- 1 cup crushed ice
- 3 tablespoons unsweetened cocoa powder
- 3 tablespoons honey

Directions:
1. In a blender, combine the bananas, almond milk, ice, cocoa powder, and honey.
2. Blend until smooth.

Nutrition:
- Calories: 219
- Protein: 2g
- Carbohydrates: 57g
- Fat: 2g

FRUIT SMOOTHIE

Total Time: 5 minutes

Preparation Time: 5 minutes
Cooking Time: 0 minutes
Servings: 2

Ingredients:
- 2 cups blueberries (or any fresh or frozen fruit, cut into pieces if the fruit is large)
- 2 cups unsweetened almond milk
- 1 cup crushed ice
- ½ teaspoon ground ginger (or other dried ground spice such as turmeric, cinnamon, or nutmeg)

Directions:
1. In a blender, combine the blueberries, almond milk, ice, and ginger.
2. Blend until smooth.

Nutrition:
- Calories: 125
- Protein: 2g
- Carbohydrates: 23g
- Fat: 4g

MANGO PEAR SMOOTHIE

Total Time: 5 minutes

Preparation Time: 5 minutes
Cooking Time: 0 minute
Servings: 1

Ingredients:
- 2 ice cubes
- ½ cup Greek yogurt, plain
- ½ mango, peeled, pitted & chopped
- 1 cup kale, chopped
- 1 pear, ripe, cored & chopped

Directions:
1. Take all ingredients and place them in your blender.
2. Blend together until thick and smooth.
3. Serve.

Nutrition:
- Calories: 350
- Protein: 40g
- Fats: 12g
- Carbohydrates: 11 g

Total Time: 5 minutes

Preparation Time: 5 minutes
Cooking Time: 0 minutes
Servings: 2

Ingredients:
- 2 cups raspberries
- ½ cup Greek yogurt
- ½ cup almond milk
- ½ tsp vanilla extract

Directions:
1. In your blender, combine the raspberries with the milk, vanilla, and the yogurt, pulse well, divide into 2 glasses and serve for breakfast.

Nutrition:
- Calories 245
- Fat: 9.5g
- Carbs: 5.6g
- Protein: 1.6g

CHIA-POMEGRANATE SMOOTHIE

Total Time: 5 minutes

Preparation Time: 5 minutes
Cooking Time: 0 minutes
Servings: 2

Ingredients:
- 1 cup pure pomegranate juice (no sugar added)
- 1 cup frozen berries
- 1 cup coarsely chopped kale
- 2 tablespoons chia seeds
- 3 Medjool dates, pitted and coarsely chopped
- Pinch ground cinnamon

Directions:
1. In a blender, combine the pomegranate juice, berries, kale, chia seeds, dates, and cinnamon and pulse until smooth.
2. Pour into glasses and serve.

Nutrition:
- Calories: 275
- Fat: 5g
- Carbohydrates: 59g
- Protein: 5g

MEDITERRANEAN MUG CAKES

Total Time: 5 minutes

Preparation Time: 5 minutes
Cooking Time: 0 minutes
Servings: 2

Ingredients
- 2 eggs
- 1 ½ tablespoons butter, melted
- 4 tablespoons full-fat milk
- 1 tablespoon rose water
- 1/4 teaspoon ground cinnamon
- 1/8 teaspoon grated nutmeg
- A pinch of coarse sea salt
- 4 tablespoons all-purpose flour
- 1/2 teaspoon baking powder
- 2 tablespoons cocoa powder
- 2 tablespoons powdered sugar
- 1 teaspoon grated orange zest

Directions:
1. Whisk the eggs, melted butter, milk, rose water, cinnamon, nutmeg, and salt.
2. Add in the flour, baking powder, cocoa powder, and sugar.
3. Spoon the batter into two mugs.
4. Microwave for 1 minute 30 seconds and top with the grated orange zest.
5. Serve.

Nutrition:
- Calories: 264
- Fat: 14.4g
- Carbs: 25.5g
- Protein: 10.1g

STRAWBERRY-RHUBARB SMOOTHIE

Total Time: 8 minutes

Preparation Time: 5 minutes
Cooking Time: 3 minutes
Servings: 1

Ingredients:
- 1 rhubarb stalk, chopped
- 1 cup sliced fresh strawberries
- ½ cup plain Greek yogurt
- 2 tablespoons honey
- Pinch ground cinnamon
- 3 ice cubes

Directions:
1. Place a small saucepan filled with water over high heat and bring to a boil.
2. Add the rhubarb and boil for 3 minutes.
3. Drain and transfer the rhubarb to a blender.
4. Add the strawberries, yogurt, honey, and cinnamon and pulse the mixture until it is smooth.
5. Add the ice and blend until thick, with no ice lumps remaining.
6. Pour the smoothie into a glass and enjoy cold.

Nutrition:
- Calories: 295
- Fat: 8g
- Carbohydrates: 56g
- Protein: 6g

Total Time: 10 minutes

Preparation Time: 5 minutes
Cooking Time: 5 minutes
Servings: 1

Ingredients:
- ½ cup frozen and unsweetened blueberries
- ½ banana slices up
- ¾ cup plain nonfat Greek yogurt
- ¾ cup unsweetened vanilla almond milk
- 2 cups of ice cubes

Directions:
1. Add all of the ingredients into a blender.
2. Blend until smooth.

Nutrition:
- Calories: 230
- Protein: 19.1 g
- Fat: 2.6 g
- Carbohydrates: 32.9 g

RASPBERRY VANILLA SMOOTHIE

Total Time: 10 minutes

Preparation Time: 5 minutes
Cooking Time: 5 minutes
Servings: 2 cups

Ingredients:
- 1 cup frozen raspberries
- 6-ounce container of vanilla Greek yogurt
- ½ cup of unsweetened vanilla almond milk

Directions:
1. Take all of your ingredients and place them in a blender.
2. Process until smooth and liquified.

Nutrition:
- Calories: 155
- Protein: 7 g
- Fat: 2 g
- Carbohydrates: 30 g

MEDITERRANEAN SMOOTHIE

Total Time: 10 minutes

Preparation Time: 5 minutes
Cooking Time: 5 minutes
Servings: 2

Ingredients:
- 2 cups of baby spinach
- 1 teaspoon fresh ginger root
- 1 frozen banana, pre-sliced
- 1 small mango
- ½ cup beet juice
- ½ cup of skim milk
- 4-6 ice cubes

Directions:
1. Take all ingredients and place them in your blender.
2. Blend together until thick and smooth.
3. Serve.

Nutrition:
- Calories: 168
- Protein: 4 g
- Fat: 1 g
- Carbohydrates: 39 g 1

GREEK FROZEN YOGURT DESSERT

Total Time: 10 minutes

Preparation Time: 10 minutes
Cooking Time: 0 minutes
Servings: 2

Ingredients
- 1/2 pineapple, diced
- 2 cups Greek-style yogurt, frozen
- 3 ounces almonds, slivered

Directions
1. Divide the pineapple between two dessert bowls.
2. Spoon the yogurt over it.
3. Top with the slivered almonds.
4. Cover and place in your refrigerator until you're ready to serve.
5. Enjoy!

Nutrition:
- Calories: 307
- Fat: 14.4g
- Carbs: 29.1g
- Protein: 18g

PISTACHIO AND TAHINI HALVA

Total Time: 15 minutes

Preparation Time: 15 minutes
Cooking Time: 0 minutes
Servings: 2

Ingredients:
- 1/2 cup water
- 1/2-pound sugar
- 10 ounces tahini, at room temperature
- A ping of sea salt
- 1/2 teaspoon vanilla paste
- 1/2 teaspoon crystal citric acid
- 1/3 cup shelled pistachios, chopped

Directions:
1. Bring the water to a full boil in a small saucepan.
2. Add in the sugar and stir. Let it cook, stirring occasionally, until a candy thermometer registers 250 degrees F. Heat off.
3. Stir in the tahini.
4. Continue to stir with a wooden spoon just until halva comes together in a smooth mass; do not overmix your halva.
5. Add in the remaining ingredients and stir again to combine well.
6. Scrape your halva into a parchment-lined square pan and smooth the top.
7. Let it cool to room temperature; cover tightly with a plastic wrap and place in your refrigerator for at least 2 hours.

Nutrition:
- Calories: 464
- Fat: 28.4g
- Carbs: 49.5g
- Protein: 9.4g

BLUEBERRY GREEK YOGURT PANCAKES

Total Time: 30 minutes

Preparation time: 15 minutes
Cooking time: 15 minutes
Servings: 6

Ingredients:
- 1 1/4 cup all-purpose flour
- 2 tsp baking powder
- 1 tsp baking soda
- 1/4 tsp salt
- 1/4 cup sugar
- 3 eggs
- 3 tbsp vegan butter unsalted, melted
- 1/2 cup milk
- 1 1/2 cups Greek yogurt plain, non-fat
- 1/2 cup blueberries optional

Toppings:
- Greek yogurt Mixed berries
- blueberries, raspberries and blackberries

Directions:
1. In a large bowl, whisk together the flour, salt, baking powder and baking soda.
2. In a separate bowl, whisk together butter, sugar, eggs, Greek yogurt, and milk until the mixture is smooth.
3. Then add in the Greek yogurt mixture from step to the dry mixture in step 1, mix to combine, allow the patter to sit for 20 minutes to get a smooth texture – if using blueberries fold them into the pancake batter.
4. Heat the pancake griddle, spray with non-stick butter spray or just brush with butter.
5. Pour the batter, in 1/4 cupful's, onto the griddle.
6. Cook until the bubbles on top burst and create small holes, lift up the corners of the pancake to see if they're golden browned on the bottom
7. With a wide spatula, flip the pancake and cook on the other side until lightly browned.

8. Serve.

Nutrition:
- Calories: 258
- Carbohydrates: 33g
- Fat: 8g
- Protein: 11g

NOTES

CPSIA information can be obtained
at www.ICGtesting.com
Printed in the USA
BVHW010623110521
606945BV00003B/299